THE VICTORIA HISTORY OF LEICESTERSHIRE

BUCKMINSTER
AND SEWSTERN

Pamela J. Fisher

VICTORIA
COUNTY
HISTORY

First published 2017

A Victoria County History publication

© The University of London, 2017

ISBN 978 1 909646 69 8

INSTITUTE OF | SCHOOL OF
HISTORICAL | ADVANCED STUDY
RESEARCH | UNIVERSITY
OF LONDON

Cover image: The Row, Buckminster. Photograph taken by Pamela J. Fisher (2015).
Back cover image: Main Street, Sewstern. Photograph taken by Pamela J. Fisher (2016).

Typeset in Minion Pro by Lianne Sherlock

CONTENTS

LIST OF ILLUSTRATIONS

We are grateful to Ron Skins for allowing us to use Figure 1, to Historic England for their permission to reproduce Figures 7 and 8, to Michael Goodacre for Figure 10, to Geoff Dunkley for Figure 13, to the Record Office for Leicestershire, Leicester and Rutland for allowing us to use Figure 16 and Map 4, to Lambeth Palace Library for their permission to include Figure 19, and to Richard Tollemache for permission to reproduce Maps 2, 5 and 6, which are in the Buckminster Estate Archive. The base for Figure 15 and Map 1 are taken from John Nichols, *History and Antiquities of the County of Leicester*, III. All other photographs are by the author, and were taken in 2015–17.

Figure

Map

THE VICTORIA COUNTY HISTORY for Leicestershire produced four substantial volumes (they are generally known as 'red books') between 1950 and 1964, but then the project to publish histories of every village and town in the county was laid aside as funding was no longer available. When a new Leicestershire Victoria County History Trust was founded in 2008 to revive and complete the work, I was pleased to become a patron. I welcomed the idea that every parish would have its history researched and published, but then realised that I could make a practical contribution by sponsoring the history of the parish, containing the two villages of Buckminster and Sewstern, with which my family has been associated since 1763.

Pam Fisher took on the task of discovering evidence from prehistoric times to the present century, and she has worked with professional expertise, helped by enthusiastic local volunteers. Now the work has been written and made ready for publication after three years of investigations, which is a tribute to Pam's dedication and inspiration. Everyone can now read about the two villages' varied and eventful past development, covering the landscape, the ownership of land, economic and social changes, including the relief of poverty and the advance of education, religious life and local government. The prominent families such as the successive lords of the manor, receive attention, but also the lives of the villagers are revealed. A particular theme is the remarkable contrast between the two villages, as Buckminster was largely agricultural and in recent centuries was strongly influenced by its lords, but with a spirit of independence the people of Sewstern pursued a wider variety of occupations.

This is a book which will be read and enjoyed by local people who will recognise the places, buildings and some of the people, but it will have a wide circulation, because the Victoria County History is a national organisation, based in London, and the history Buckminster and Sewstern will be made available throughout this country and overseas. It gives me great pleasure and satisfaction that the history of these two attractive and interesting villages will be better known in Leicestershire and beyond its boundaries.

Lyonel Tollemache

Sir Lyonel Tollemache
July 2017

ACKNOWLEDGEMENTS

WHEN I BEGAN RESEARCHING this parish history I was surprised that so little has been written about these villages. I had driven through Buckminster a few times before, pondered the 'minster' element within the place-name and noted the estate cottages. Sewstern was completely unknown to me, although I was aware of the ancient track known as Sewstern Lane. Researching and writing this parish history has been an immensely enjoyable voyage of discovery, in which I have come to know not just the villages, but also many of their inhabitants, and have made new friends.

I owe a huge debt of gratitude to many people. This book has been written only through the generous financial support given to Leicestershire Victoria County History Trust by Sir Lyonel Tollemache, and through his practical support for the project, including access to the estate archive. When we first met, the Victoria County History had not published anything in Leicestershire since 1964, and both the Trust and I are exceedingly grateful for his confidence and support. Other members of the Tollemache family have also been supportive, especially Sir Lyonel's wife Mary, their son Richard, and daughter Katheryne. They have put me in touch with former residents, provided me with facts and figures about the estate today and supported the talks and exhibition I arranged.

Throughout this research, I have benefited greatly from numerous discussions with Chris Dyer of the University of Leicester. He has provided me with wise advice, helpful suggestions and constructive criticism over an extended period, for which I offer my grateful thanks. I also thank Helen Nicolson of Cardiff University, who generously provided me with a transcript of the relevant parts of the accounts of the Templars' estates, and Thomas Cogswell of the University of California, who pointed me towards documents in the Huntington Library that I would otherwise not have read.

Leicestershire Victoria County History Trust works in partnership with local people to produce its research. Within Buckminster and Sewstern, Jill Arnold, Jill Barthorpe, Ian Bracey, Rachel Dearden, Heather Exton, David Featherstone, Elizabeth and Michael Goodacre, Alan Hart, Emma Hatherley, Jed Jaggard, Claire Kurth, Brian and Margaret Lowe, Alan McPherson, Penny and Richard Vincent, Sylvia Whitney and Ann Wild have assisted in many different ways, including welcoming me into their homes, reading and analysing locally-held archives, generously sharing their own previous research, local knowledge, memories and archaeological discoveries, and providing access to buildings, documents and old photographs. This book has benefited enormously from their involvement, and I thank them all for their support and help. I hope the others will forgive me for singling out Michael and Elizabeth Goodacre for my especial thanks, as they provided extensive help in each of those ways, have let me use their dining room as a study on several visits and lent me many boxes and bags of deeds, documents and photographs, including hundreds of transcripts of newspaper articles painstakingly typed out several years ago by Mike Reed, to whom I also owe my thanks.

At Buckminster School, Jon Brown, Debbie Clarke, Kate Parkin and their colleagues kindly allowed me to introduce many of the children to aspects of the history of the two villages, helped to produce material for an exhibition and let me borrow the historic school log books. I am grateful to them all, and to the children for their interest and questions. My warm thanks are also proffered to Carol Cambers, who kindly shared her expertise and helped me to devise the school project, and to Helen Sharp of Leicestershire Museums, who kindly lent me a selection of archaeological finds from the parish to show the children and to display at the exhibition.

The twentieth century can be difficult to research, but my task was made easier by former residents Gillian Dexter, Geoff Dunkley, Betty Neal, Roy Rayson, David Rudkin and Ron Skins, and I thank them all for sharing with me their photographs and vivid memories of living in these villages. I am also grateful to Sue Blaxland, who kindly shared her detailed research into the walled garden at Buckminster Hall, and to Aileen and Peter Ball, Chris Bursnall and David Hibbit, who crossed the county boundary from Lincolnshire to lend their time, archaeological expertise and equipment in the search for Sewstern's lost medieval chapel.

The core of the research has utilised documents held in many different repositories, as well as the Buckminster Estate Office. I am very grateful to The Duke of Rutland for arranging for me to receive images of documents held at Belvoir Castle, to Andrew Norman for admitting me to the archives at Rockingham Castle and to Peter Foden and Basil Morgan for their help. As a frequent visitor to the Record Office for Leicestershire, Leicester and Rutland, I have come to know most of the archivists and staff there, and thank them for their very friendly and efficient service, producing even the most obscure documents, and assisting with queries. My thanks are also tendered to the archivists and staff at The National Archives, the Church of England Records Centre, the Huntington Library in California, John Rylands Library in Manchester, Lambeth Palace Library, the Victoria and Albert Museum, the county record offices in Lincolnshire, Northamptonshire, Nottinghamshire and Surrey and at the David Wilson Library at the University of Leicester. Without exception, they have all been unfailingly helpful. With so many documents to read, I am also immensely grateful for the assistance of Anne Bryan, Helen Edwards and Delia Richards, who have transcribed numerous 17th-century and other records for me, Susan Kilby and Matt Tompkins, who provided help with medieval documents and Carolyn Paisley who helped to transcribe other material. I also thank the University of Leicester for providing me with office space and IT facilities.

I also tender my grateful thanks to the anonymous academic reviewer of this text for his or her helpful comments, Cath D'Alton for the excellent cartography and Matt Bristow, Adam Chapman, Jessica Davies and Lianne Sherlock at the Central Office of the Victoria County History in London, whose friendly advice and support over many months, in transforming my text into this book, has been outstanding. That they are mentioned last reflects only the chronology of producing this book. Any errors that remain in the text or maps are entirely my own.

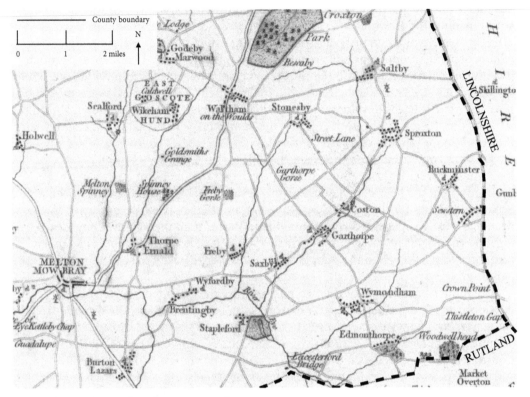

Map 1 *John Cary's map of north-east Leicestershire in 1795.*

THE PARISH OF BUCKMINSTER is in north-east Leicestershire. Its eastern border is also the county boundary with Lincolnshire, and the unitary authority (former county) of Rutland lies one mile south of the parish. The nearest towns are Melton Mowbray, nine miles to the west, Grantham (Lincs.), 11 miles north, and Oakham (Rutl.), 12 miles south. There were closer markets in the Middle Ages at Waltham on the Wolds (granted 1219), Wymondham (granted 1303), and Market Overton (Rutl., from 1200), all within six miles.[1]

The parish contains the two villages of Buckminster and Sewstern, the former occupying the higher ground in the north of the parish, with Sewstern one mile to its south-east (Map 1). They became separate civil parishes in 1866, but were reunited within a single parish in 1936.[2] The parish name includes the Old English personal

1 S. Letters, 'Gazetteer of fairs and markets', http://www.history.ac.uk/cmh/gaz/gazweb2.html (accessed 21 Sept. 2016).
2 F. Youngs, *Local Administrative Units: Northern England* (1991), 223.

name Bucca, and its suffix implies a minster stood here, or was supported by this land,[1] although no physical evidence of an important early church is visible. Sewstern's place-name also incorporates an Old English personal name, and probably means Saewig's thorn-patch.[2]

Despite their proximity, a common administrative history and similar soil types, the two villages have been markedly different in character for many centuries. In 1086, Buckminster's families were mostly free, while most of Sewstern's residents owed feudal services to their lord.[3] By 1381, some of Sewstern's inhabitants had taken advantage of their position near Sewstern Lane, which marked the county boundary with Lincolnshire, and the village had developed a commercial character. Several residents were craftsmen or traders, in contrast to Buckminster, whose people were wholly dependent upon agriculture for their living.[4] Surviving 17th-century probate inventories demonstrate that Buckminster was still a purely agricultural village, while several of Sewstern's residents followed a trade, usually alongside a little farming.[5] As a result, the two villages developed separate experiences of poverty, as shown within the lay subsidies (taxes) of the 16th century, the hearth taxes of the late 17th century and the cost of poor relief in the 19th century.[6]

Tensions sometimes arose between the villages. In 1550, for example, Buckminster's residents sought to make it clear that they had not been party to the decision to sell the bell from Sewstern's medieval chapel without the king's licence.[7] Separate charities for the poor of Buckminster and those of Sewstern suggest that residents strongly identified with their village, rather than the parish. They joined together to provide a parish workhouse in 1809, but that arrangement broke down just nine years later, when the people of Buckminster resolved to sell their share of the building.[8]

The modern characters of the two villages have been shaped by transport developments and the pattern of land ownership. From the 1840s, the droving trade along Sewstern Lane ceased, as livestock began to be transported by rail. Sewstern became a rural backwater, with little non-agricultural employment other than ironstone quarrying between the 1890s (in neighbouring Lincolnshire parishes) and 1968.[9] Horses were ridden for pleasure along its peaceful roads in 2017, even on weekday mornings.[10] Buckminster was never on a turnpike road, but its position astride the main road linking Melton Mowbray to the A1 trunk road at Colsterworth has brought significant traffic through the village since the motor engine made longer journeys more attractive.

1   B. Cox, *The Place-names of Leicestershire*, II (Nottingham, 2002), 54.
2   Cox, *Place-names*, 58–9.
3   *Domesday*, 630, 643.
4   *Poll Taxes 1377–81*, (ed.) Fenwick, I, 600, 603.
5   Below, 59.
6   Below, 63–5.
7   Below, 65, 87.
8   Below, 74.
9   Below, 55–8.
10   Observed by the author on several visits in 2015–17.

Figure 1 *Main Street, Buckminster in 1948, looking north-east from the junction with Sproxton Road. The house in the foreground (Stonelea) is one of the few limestone buildings in the village. The building on the right is the general stores and former petrol station.*

The built character of Buckminster changed substantially from the 1790s, when William Manners (baronet from 1793) decided to move to the village and increase his landholdings around his new country house, Buckminster Hall. Few houses survive from an earlier date, but two exceptions suggest that earlier properties were built from limestone (Fig. 1). Later houses are mostly built from brick. Unusually for a small village, these include a terrace of 17 early 19th-century houses, built around the curve of Main Street (cover image), which helps them to look homely, rather than austere. Other properties mostly reflect estate improvements made between 1880 and 1935 by William Tollemache, the 9th earl of Dysart and great-grandson of Sir William Manners, which included building larger properties with gardens. Common stylistic features and the adoption of a limited palette for their paintwork identifies these as estate properties. In 2017, all the farmland, commercial and residential properties in the village were owned by the Tollemache family.

Sir William Manners also owned farmland and houses in Sewstern in 1793,[11] but he and his descendants had a limited interest in land and property acquisition in that village. The village grew organically, and the style, size and paintwork of its properties mostly reflect the individual tastes of different freeholders. The predominant building material was local limestone, quarried just across the county boundary in Lincolnshire. Much of the farmland but only some of the houses in Sewstern were owned by the Tollemache family in 2017.

11   Lincs. Arch., BRA 1189/2/23.

Parish Extent and Boundaries

The parish is broadly rectangular, and in 2011 contained 1,237 ha. (3,057 a.) of land.[12] The civil parish boundary which separated Buckminster and Sewstern in 1866 broadly followed the earlier boundary between the fields of the two villages (Map 7).[13] In 1931, shortly before reunification of the parish, Buckminster civil parish contained 1,964 a. and Sewstern contained 1,117 a.[14]

Sewstern Lane was almost certainly the original eastern boundary of the parish, and the ancient county boundary separating Leicestershire and Lincolnshire between Rutland and Harston, a distance of ten miles. The county boundary does not deviate from the lane in maps by John Prior (1777),[15] John Cary (Map 1),[16] or the first Ordnance Survey

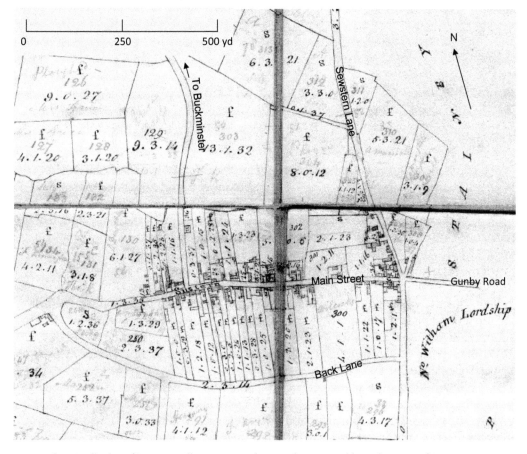

Map 2 *John Wood's plan of Sewstern village in 1829, showing the manorial boundary east of Sewstern Lane.*

12   http://neighbourhood.statistics.gov.uk/dissemination/LeadKeyFigures (accessed 1 Jun. 2016).
13   Below, 43.
14   Census, 1931.
15   ROLLR, Ma/L/31.
16   ROLLR, MA/L/12; Nichols, *History*, II, between 6 and 7.

drafts (1815).[17] However, and referring to two separate anomalies, Nichols recorded in 1795 that, 'Two or three houses in Sewstern are in the county of Lincoln; and one on the very boundary itself, a part of it in Leicestershire, the other part in Lincolnshire.'[18] The 'Two or three houses' mentioned were immediately to the south-east of the crossroads where Gunby Road crosses Sewstern Lane to become Main Street, Sewstern, and lay within a detached part of North Witham parish (Lincs.). There were three houses here by 1563, when they were described as being in 'Shester' in North Witham.[19] They may have originated as cottages built on wasteland, whose occupants found they could earn a living from people passing along the lane. They were occupied by three people in 1577, who were regarded by North Witham's parson John Davie as being 'in my parish at Sewstern'.[20] This land became part of Gunby parish (Lincs.) in 1887.[21] Following a further boundary change, it was incorporated within Buckminster parish (and Leicestershire) in 1965 (Map 3).[22]

The existence of a house 'on the very boundary' is curious. It stood north-east of the crossroads, on the edge of a triangle of land east of Sewstern Lane containing c.13 a. This land was within the manor of Buckminster and Sewstern in 1829 (Map 2), and within Sewstern's township boundary in 1840.[23] An Ordnance Survey boundary survey of 1883 shows the parish and county boundaries passing through a corner of what was then the Red Lion Inn.[24] Specifically, it passed through a coursed limestone wall containing a fireplace apparently of the late 16th or early 17th century.[25] This property may have been deliberately built across the boundary, which would imply that that the county boundary had veered away from the lane by at least the early 17th century.

In 2016, the southern parish boundary left Sewstern Lane at a track 1¼ miles south of the village, and ran almost due west for 2½ miles, before picking up the fossilised edges of former open-field furlongs for the final mile to reach a small brook. Field names in the south-east of the parish contain the word 'moor',[26] and this part of the boundary may have been laid out across uncultivated land. After following the course of the brook north for a quarter of a mile, the boundary continued north for 2 miles by a series of large dog legs, picking up another section of brook for part of its journey, but otherwise interlocking with the former open field furlongs of Coston. Upon reaching a minor road from Sproxton, the boundary turned to take an almost straight line north-east for 2 miles to return to Sewstern Lane, following the contours, but slightly to the north of, the foot of a small dale containing Cringle Brook.

17 ROLLR, OS survey, 266.
18 Nichols, *History*, II, 129.
19 A. Dyer and D.M. Palliser (eds), *The Diocesan Population Returns for 1563 and 1603* (Oxford, 2005), 192.
20 Lincs. Arch., Lincoln Consistory Court wills, I, ff. 82v–83v; *South Witham Archaeological Group, The History of the Parish of North Witham and Lobthorpe* (South Witham, c.2007), 92.
21 http://www.visionofbritain.org.uk/unit/10422243 (accessed 7 Mar. 2015).
22 East Midlands Counties Order 1965, http://www.visionofbritain.org.uk/unit/10422280 (accessed 7 Mar. 2015).
23 Buckminster Estate Arch., Lordships map; ROLLR, Ti/279/1.
24 TNA, OS 26/5615.
25 The building has been converted to a private house, and the author is grateful to Jill Barthorpe (owner) for showing her the interior.
26 ROLLR, Ti/279/1.

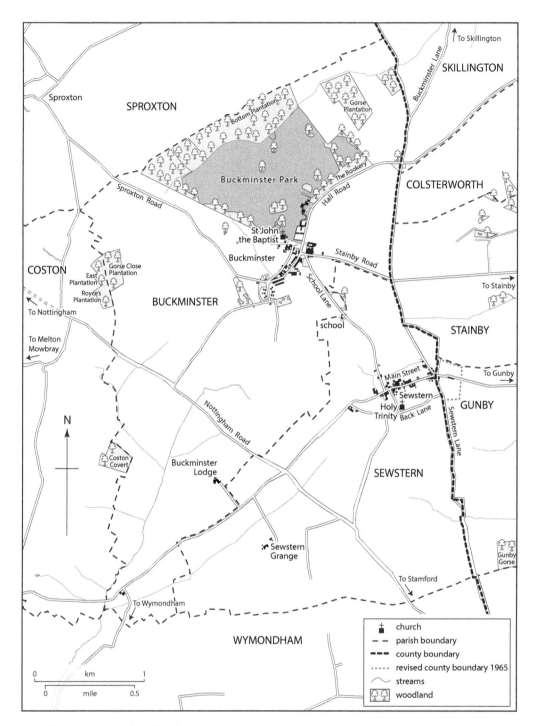

Map 3 *The separate parishes of Buckminster and Sewstern in 1887, also showing the 1965 revision to the county boundary.*

The internal township boundary (Map 7) was complex and included detached portions of land.[27] It was presumably designed to share the natural resources of the parish between the two villages, including the streams and an area of heathland in the north. The boundary created between the civil parishes of Buckminster and Sewstern in 1866 (Map 3) broadly followed the earlier township boundary on its diagonal course north-eastwards from a point half a mile east of the south-west corner of the parish to reach Stainby Road, east of Buckminster village. It then ran east along Stainby Road to meet Sewstern Lane; the Sewstern land formerly to the north of Stainby Road was transferred to Buckminster.[28]

Physical Characteristics

Buckminster village occupies the highest ground within the parish, on the northern edge of an escarpment which stands a little over 500 ft above sea level. To the east, the land slopes gently down to the Lincolnshire fenland and the Wash, 37 miles away. Westwards, the land dips away before climbing to the north Leicestershire wolds at Waltham, 6 miles away and 60 ft higher than Buckminster. The parish stands on the watershed between the river basins of the Trent and Witham, which is almost coincident with the county boundary.[29] The three small streams which rise in the south-west of the parish flow south before converging and joining the river Eye, which eventually flows into the Trent. The small stream which rises in the south-east of Sewstern, and Cringle Brook, which rises in the north of the parish, flow into the river Witham.

The limestone for the buildings and walls within the parish probably came from Lincolnshire quarries near Gunby, but hint at the underlying geology, which resulted in a reshaping of the landscape in the 20th century through quarrying. The western edge of the Northampton Sand Bed, the lowest of the oolitic beds, snakes across the central and eastern part of the parish.[30] It was between 7 and 12 ft thick, and rich in iron. Above was an overburden of between 3 and 15 ft,[31] comprising a thin layer of poor-quality limestone sandwiched between lower estuarine clay and upper deposits of boulder clay.[32] Open cast quarrying for ironstone took place on a rolling basis across the parish between 1935 and 1968, with the land restored to agricultural use within a season (Map 8). In the quarried area, the roads and the curtilages of the buildings acted as quarry boundaries, and stand up to 12 ft proud of the restored land.

The land within the parish to the west of this is mostly covered with boulder clay, with lighter heathland soils in the extreme north of the parish.[33] Near Stainby Road, in the east of the parish, there is a small area of marlstone, which gave rise to 'red earth' names for the closes.[34] The heavy land, coupled with inclosure for pasture in c.1600,

27   Below, 43; ROLLR, Ti/53/1; Ti/279/1.
28   OS map, 6", Leics. XXI.NW (1884 edn); Leics. XXI.NE (1884 edn); Leics. XIV.SE (1884 edn).
29   A. Fox, *A Lost Frontier Revealed: Regional Separation in the East Midlands* (Hatfield, 2009), 17.
30   Geological Survey of Great Britain, *The Northampton Sand Ironstone, Stratigraphy, Structure and Reserves* (1951), Plates II–IV.
31   TNA, HLG 132/370; H.B. Hewlett, *The Quarries: Ironstone, Limestone and Sand* (Oakham, 1979), 25.
32   TNA, HLG 132/370, cross section detail from boreholes; HLG 89/783.
33   http://mapapps.bgs.ac.uk/geologyofbritain/home.html (accessed 8 Mar. 2016).
34   Lincs. Arch., REEVE 1/12/1/8; DIOC/TER BUNDLE/LEICS/BUCKMINSTER/1700.

preserved much of the ridge and furrow of the medieval arable fields until the mid-20th century,[35] but this had largely been lost by 2017, from quarrying and a return to arable farming. There were brickworks near Buckminster village, with later landscaping work creating artificial fishing lakes.

No woodland was recorded in either manor in 1086,[36] but trees formed a prominent landscape feature in 2017. Large areas of mixed woodland stood to the north and east of the park, with smaller areas behind The Crescent and on the south-western park boundary. Trees grew alongside many of the hedgerows, small copses filled the corners of some fields, providing cover for game birds, foxes and other wildlife,[37] and there were specimen trees on the village green.

Communication

Roads

There are three important north–south routes in the vicinity of the parish (Map 4).[38] Sewstern Lane is almost certainly the earliest of these. Archaeologists are wary of assigning dates to roads where there is no evidence of construction,[39] but its route, adopting a series of gentle curves across high ground, and the lack of villages along the way (Sewstern is an exception) suggest it may have been a prehistoric track, linking the river Welland near Stamford (Lincs.) to the Trent near Newark (Notts.). It coincides with parish and county boundaries for more than ten miles, indicating that it was a clear landscape feature when these were drawn. Four miles north of Buckminster it was known as Schirestrete (Shire Street) in 1258.[40] There is no evidence to support a mooted Bronze Age origin.[41] The southernmost section of its assumed original length, from Stamford almost to Greetham (Rutl.), became a Roman road (Ermine Street). The next section to the northern boundary of Rutland, near Thistleton, may also have been adopted by the Romans: it runs straight and a short section stands almost 3 ft proud of the neighbouring land, in the manner of a Roman agger. These hints of 'Romanization' disappear to the north of Thistleton.[42] Including the verges, the section running alongside the parish is 24 m. wide (Fig. 2).

35   R.F. Hartley, *The Medieval Earthworks of North-East Leicestershire* (Leicester, 1987), 63, 68–9.
36   *Domesday*, 630, 643.
37   OS Map 25", Leics. XIV.14 (1885 edn); XIV.15 (1888 edn); XX1.3 (1888 edn), and see 00 (Economic History).
38   ROLLR, Misc. 2a.
39   C. Taylor, *Roads and Tracks of Britain* (Guildford, 1979), 22–39; B.P. Hindle, *Roads, Tracks and their Interpretation* (1993), 16–27; P. Fowler, 'Moving through the landscape', in P. Everson and T. Williamson (eds), *The Archaeology of Landscape* (Manchester, 1998), 26–32.
40   Nichols, *History*, II, App, 81, citing a survey of land belonging to Croxton abbey, whereabouts unknown.
41   W.G. Hoskins, *The Making of the English Landscape* (1965 impression), 187, 189.
42   I.D. Margary, *Roman Roads in Britain* (1967 edn), 223–4, 227.

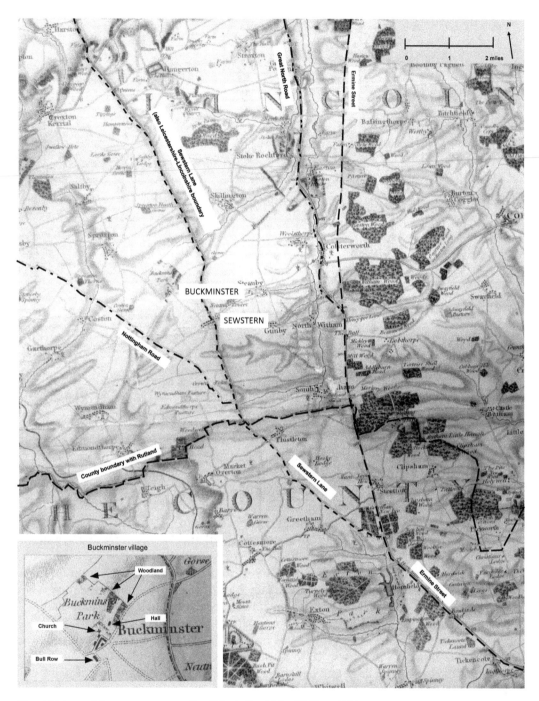

Map 4 'A tract of the country surrounding Belvoir Castle', by W. King, 1806.

Figure 2 *Sewstern Lane in 2017, between Stainby Road and Hall Road, looking north.*

Ermine Street, passing to the east of the parish boundary, was the main long-distance route north in the Roman period. It turned north-east, away from Sewstern Lane, near Greetham, and passed to the east of Colsterworth (Lincs.), on its way to Lincoln. By the 12th century, this Roman road had been superseded by the Great North Road. This followed the route of Ermine Street from Stamford almost to Colsterworth, but then branched west to pass through Colsterworth and Grantham (Lincs.), rejoining Sewstern Lane at Long Bennington (Lincs.), six miles south of Newark.[43]

Sewstern Lane remained convenient for some travellers. It was almost certainly used by Edward I and his retinue in 1301 as they travelled from Lincoln to the royal palace at Woodstock (Oxon.), a journey which included overnight stops at Grantham, Buckminster and Oakham.[44] The range of occupations present in Sewstern in 1381 suggest it remained an important route. It continued to facilitate contact between Buckminster residents and tradesmen in Stamford through the Middle Ages,[45] and was suitable for the carriage of large and heavy loads, as suggested by the sale of the bell from Sewstern's chapel to a Stamford pewterer in 1550.[46]

43   D. Stocker, *England's Landscape: The East Midlands* (2006), 32.
44   E.W. Safford, *Itinerary of Edward I*, pt II, L&I Soc., 132 (1976), 170.
45   *Poll Taxes 1377–81*, (ed.) Fenwick, I, 600.
46   TNA, SC 2/183/154, m. 1d.

In the 18th and 19th centuries Sewstern Lane provided an alternative route when the section of the Great North Road between Grantham and Stamford became subject to turnpike tolls in 1739.[47] It is probably in this period that it became known as The Drift, reflecting its use by drovers taking livestock from Scotland and northern England to distant markets, especially London, to avoid the tolls and delays of the turnpike.[48] Its width (including verges) was ideally suited to this purpose (Fig. 2). In 2017, Sewstern Lane was only a green lane to the north of Hall Road.

Another early road (much of it a green lane in 2017) leaves the 'Romanized' section of Sewstern Lane near Thistleton to run north-west across the parish, through Waltham on the Wolds and on to Nottingham. The section near Stonesby is labelled Street Lane in Prior's county map of 1777,[49] but there is no older evidence for this name, or for the alternative of King Street Lane, used by some local people.[50] The section through Buckminster was known as Nottingham Road or Nottingham Highway in the 17th and early 18th centuries.[51] Although almost straight, no section of this road has been identified as Roman in origin, and it does not lead to Roman towns. It is mostly ignored along its length by parish boundaries, and with the important fair towns of Nottingham and Stamford at each end, an early medieval date may be more likely.[52]

The turnpike road from Melton Mowbray to the Great North Road did not pass through the parish, but went through Waltham on the Wolds to Grantham.[53] This remained the main route in the 20th and early 21st century, although the opening of a service area on the A1 trunk road at Colsterworth in 1989 encouraged vehicles travelling from Melton to take the road to Colsterworth, which passes along Main Street, Buckminster.[54]

Back Lane in Sewstern, and the road from Sewstern to Wymondham, are wide and also ideally suited to driving livestock. They may have originated as livestock routes between Sewstern Lane and the medieval market in Wymondham, or transhumance routes from Sewstern village via Nottingham Road to possible common upland grazing at Waltham on the Wolds. The verges may have been rented out by the manor to landless villagers, sojourners and drovers, for grazing. These roads still carried very little traffic in 2017.

47   12 Geo. II, c. 8.
48   *VCH Leics.* II, 78; Stocker, *England's Landscape*, 31–2.
49   ROLLR, Ma/L/1. See also Map 1.
50   Fox, *Lost Frontier*, 155.
51   Lincs. Arch., DIOC/TER/5 f. 168; DIOC/TER BUNDLE/LEICS/BUCKMINSTER/1605; DIOC/
     TER 13/70; DIOC/TER BUNDLE/LEICS/BUCKMINSTER/1700; DIOC/TER BUNDLE/LEICS/
     BUCKMINSTER/1703; DIOC/TER BUNDLE/LEICS/BUCKMINSTER/1724; DIOC/TER BUNDLE/
     LEICS/BUCKMINSTER/1745; ROLLR, 1D 41/2/111; ROLLR 1D 41/2/113.
52   Margary, *Roman Roads*; *VCH Leics.* II, 67, 78.
53   20 Geo. III, c. 95.
54   http://motorwayservicesonline.co.uk/Colsterworth (accessed 4 Sept. 2016).

Carriers and Buses

Carriers ran between Melton Mowbray and Grantham from at least 1822, calling at Buckminster.[55] There was a weekly service from the villages to Melton on Tuesdays and Grantham on Saturdays between the 1840s and 1920s.[56] By 1932 there were daily buses to Melton, Grantham and Oakham.[57] In 2017, the 'Hail and Ride' service operated by Centrebus ran one return journey each day between Melton Mowbray and Grantham, calling at Buckminster and Sewstern.[58]

Railways

Other than the short-lived industrial railways which served the quarries between 1935 and 1964,[59] there has never been a railway in the parish. A station opened in 1848 at Whissendine (Rutl.), five miles south-east of Buckminster, on the Syston and Peterborough Railway; it closed in 1955.[60] One mile closer, Edmondthorpe and Wymondham station, on the Midland Railway's Saxby and Bourne branch line, opened for goods in 1893 and passengers in 1894, closing in 1959.[61] Proposed railways from Leicester to Boston (Lincs.) in 1845,[62] and Saxby to Skegness (Lincs.) in 1888,[63] would have passed through the parish, but both schemes lacked sufficient support to be built.[64]

Observation Posts for National Security

The Melton Mowbray town wardens contributed 5s. in 1597 towards the cost of a beacon in Buckminster, as part of England's coastal defences during the Anglo-Spanish War (1585–1604).[65] It presumably stood on Beacon Hill, which can be identified in 1679 at the northern end of the road later known as School Lane.[66] When the country returned to war against Spain in 1625, repairs were ordered to the beacon's broken pole and the 'ruinated and decayed' watch-tower, at a cost of £85. It formed part of a chain of beacons from the east coast. A 24-hour watch was to be kept, and the beacon lit if the next beacon in the chain was seen, to summon Leicestershire's militia to go to the aid of

55 Pigot & Co., *Dir. of Leics.* (1822), 230.
56 See, for example, W. White, *Hist., Gaz. and Dir. of Leics. and Rutl.* (Sheffield, 1846), 227–8; *PO Dir. Leics. and Rutl.* (1855), 22; W. White, *Hist., Gaz. and Dir. of Leics. and Rutl.* (Sheffield, 1863), 344; W. White, *Hist., Gaz. and Dir. of Leics. and Rutl.* (Sheffield, 1877), 589; C.N. Wright, *Dir. of Leics.* (1887–8), 368; *Kelly's Dir. Leics. and Rutl.* (1895), 46; *Kelly's Dir. Leics. and Rutl.* (1916), 50; *Kelly's Dir. Leics. and Rutl.* (1908), 51; *Kelly's Dir. Leics. and Rutl.* (1928), 53.
57 *Kelly's Dir. of Leics. and Rutl.* (1932), 53.
58 https://bustimes.org.uk/localities/N0065284 (accessed 25 Jul. 2017).
59 Below, 55–8.
60 *PO Dir. Leics. and Rutl.* (1855), 22; http://www.pastscape.org.uk/hob.aspx?hob_id=509109 (accessed 3 Apr. 2015).
61 A. Moore, *Leicestershire Stations: An Historical Perspective* (Narborough, 1998), 69.
62 ROLLR, QS 73/64; QS 73/66.
63 CERC, NS/7/1/2206; ROLLR, QS 73/277.
64 *Grantham Jnl*, 24 Aug. 1889.
65 ROLLR, DG36/284/19 (entry 13 Jan. 1596/7).
66 ROLLR, 1D 41/2/111 (1679); 1D 41/2/113 (1694), Ti, 53/1; Lincs. Arch., DIOC/TER BUNDLE/LEICS/BUCKMINSTER/1700; Lincs. Arch., DIOC/TER BUNDLE/LEICS/BUCKMINSTER/1703.

Lincolnshire.[67] Rather than constructing a separate watch-tower, the watch was kept at the top of Buckminster's church tower, where a fireplace and chimney were installed.[68]

A government monitoring post was established within the parish during the Second World War, south-west of Buckminster village, and land was purchased by the government for a Royal Observer Corps post in 1953.[69] Further land was purchased by the government in 1959 for an underground nuclear monitoring station.[70] This opened in 1961, to give warning of an air attack, and to measure any radioactive fall-out. It was decommissioned in 1991, and restored as a heritage site in 2012.[71]

Post and Telecommunications

Buckminster and Sewstern both received mail by foot-post from Colsterworth from 1848. A post office opened in Buckminster in 1854, but closed in 1863.[72] It had reopened on Back Street by 1881,[73] moved to Main Street in 1983,[74] and closed in 2008, replaced for a short period by a weekly visit from a mobile office.[75] Sewstern post office opened in 1896 in the house of wheelwright and farmer Thomas Sharp.[76] It closed in 1924, but a post office reopened in 1932,[77] closing again in 2000.[78] Members of the Laxton family ran the office from 1901 to 1924, and from 1932 until the 1950s.[79]

The 9th earl of Dysart took 'a very deep interest in telephony', and supported a Grantham borough council scheme in 1900 for a municipal telephone system, with a rural line to Buckminster, but the scheme was abandoned.[80] Wealthier residents in both villages had telephones by the 1930s.[81] A new telephone exchange was built in Buckminster in 1978.[82] Buckminster Estates established Buckminster Broadband in 2010, which provided fast internet connectivity across an area of 70 square miles, including

67   Huntington Libr., HAM 53(6), ff. 164–167v.
68   Both chimney and fireplace were extant in 2016.
69   TNA, AIR 2/19472, letter 22 Jan. 1954.
70   TNA, AIR 2/19472, letter 12 Oct. 1959.
71   http://www.subbrit.org.uk/rsg/roc/db/988730925.003001.html (accessed 14 May 2016); Leics. and Rutl. HER, MLE 16028; http://www.buckminster.co.uk/buckminster-cold-war-bunker-opening/ (accessed 9 Apr. 2015).
72   J. Soer, *The Royal Mail in Leicestershire and Rutland* (1997), 64.
73   TNA, RG 14/19354/0005.
74   Soer, *The Royal Mail*, 65.
75   http://www.royalmailgroup.com/cy/decisions-leicestershire-northamptonshire-and-rutland-post-office%C2%AE-branches-announced; http://www.framlandmissionpartnership.com/Pages/SouthFramlandBenefice.aspx (accessed 3 Apr. 2015).
76   *Grantham Jnl*, 8 Feb. 1896.
77   Soer, *Royal Mail*, 224.
78   K. Smith, UK Post Offices list by county, https://79f21e9d-a-62cb3a1a-s-sites.googlegroups.com/site/ukpostofficesbycounty/home/england/Leicestershire (accessed 17 May 2016).
79   Soer, *Royal Mail*, 224.
80   Lincs. Arch., Grantham Borough 5/8, 268, 288, 439; *Grantham Jnl*, 19 Oct. 1901.
81   *Kelly's Dir. of Leics. and Rutl.* (1936), 51.
82   *Leic. Merc.*, 7 Jul. 1978.

Buckminster, Sewstern and 13 other villages in Leicestershire and Lincolnshire, through a combination of fibre optic cables and wireless transmission.[83]

Settlement

Both villages are located by springs, where the oolitic scarp meets clay. There has been little archaeological investigation, and opencast ironstone quarrying may have destroyed some evidence of early settlement. A possible Iron Age quern has been found in the south-west of the parish,[84] and it has been suggested that a nearby mound in a hedge might be a barrow,[85] but no field-walking finds have been recorded.[86] There has only been one excavation, to the west of School Lane, immediately ahead of quarrying, which uncovered eight sherds of Roman pottery, some fragments of Roman tiles and a medieval monastic grange site.[87]

Buckminster

Buckminster's houses are mostly brick, although a few larger and older properties are of coursed limestone. All of the houses are within a conservation area designated in 1973, but the only listed buildings are the church, mausoleum and old vicarage, the latter much altered and enlarged since it was built in c.1817.[88]

The village's streets trace the highest ground in the parish. St John the Baptist church is set back, to the north of the village, with the vicarage immediately to its south. Buckminster Park, where Sir William Manners built the Hall in the 1790s, is to the north of the church, and probably contains the site of the medieval manor house.[89] Only three houses in the village may have been built before 1800: a three-storey brick-built shop on Back Street, an attractive coursed-limestone property on Main Street (Stonelea, Fig. 1) and the 'Old Manor', which is built at right-angles to Back Street and faces south. The latter appears to be the oldest house in the village, and was probably built as a farmhouse, perhaps in the 17th or early 18th century; its name was adopted in the 20th century.[90] It is also built of coursed limestone, with a door and porch at the east end of the property. Records suggest there was little wood in this area,[91] and it is likely that most of the earlier houses in the village (which have not survived) were also built from limestone.

83   Inf. from Richard Tollemache [2017]; http://www.buckminsterbroadband.co.uk/ (accessed 14 May 2016).
84   Leics. and Rutl. HER, MLE 8305.
85   'Reports of Fieldwork, 1981', *Trans LAHS*, 56 (1980–81), 118; Leics. and Rutl. HER, MLE 16768.
86   Leics. and Rutl. HER (at 10 Apr. 2014).
87   D.J. Rudkin, 'The excavation of an early medieval site at Buckminster, Leicestershire', *Trans LAHS*, 47 (1970–71), 1–13; Leics. and Rutl. HER, MLE 7963; MLE 3466; see Landownership, 00.
88   Melton Mowbray BC, Conservation Area Appraisal, http://www.melton.gov.uk/downloads/file/802/buckminsterpdf (accessed 15 May 2016); NHL, no. 1061281, Ch. of St John the Baptist, Church Drive; no. 1360830, Dysart Mausoleum and railing, Church Drive; no. 1061282, The Old Vicarage, Church Drive (all accessed 20 Apr. 2014).
89   Below, 34–5.
90   ROLLR, DE 1761/15/6.
91   Below, 53.

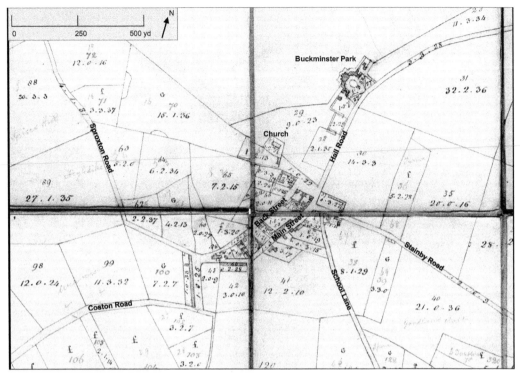

Map 5 *John Wood's plan of Buckminster village in 1829.*

Some houses were probably removed when the Hall was built. Cary's map of 1795 (Map 1) shows buildings along the road later renamed Hall Road, but these were no longer there in 1806. Their residents may have been offered a house in Bull Row, a terrace of 35 one-bedroomed houses built by 1806 on the approach to the village from the south.[92] They were probably the basis for Humphry Repton including 'the roads near … Buckminster [Park]' in 1803, when he listed examples of landowners who had provided 'comfortable workers' cottages' in the vicinity of their great house.[93] It was probably started between 1793 and 1801, and completed by 1811, as the census shows that 13 houses were built in Buckminster between 1801 and 1811.[94] A further 18 houses were built between 1821 and 1831,[95] almost certainly including Cow Row (later renamed The Row), a terrace of 17 brick cottages on the east side of Main Street (front cover). Both Bull Row and Cow Row were made available to Grantham freemen in the 1820s, and the latter may have been built for that purpose. A few other large properties were built by 1829, and would have housed senior estate staff.

92   Nichols, *History*, II, between 6 and 7; ROLLR, Misc 2a; *Royal Commission on Labour* (Parl. Papers 1893–4 [C.6894–1], xxxv), p. 139.
93   H. Repton, *Observations on the Theory and Practice of Landscape Gardening including some remarks on Grecian and Gothic architecture collected from various manuscripts in the possession of the different noblemen and gentlemen for whose use they were originally written* (London, 1803), 142–3; H. Repton, *The Art of Landscape Gardening* (1907), 173–4.
94   Census, 1801; 1811.
95   Census, 1821; 1831.

South-east of the church is a large village green, registered as such in 1969.[96] An undated sketch of *c*.1814 shows a 'Waste or Town Green' abutting the vicarage garden,[97] but its full extent was not shown. Hull Lane ran east-west immediately south of the vicarage in 1605.[98] It was 'bought by Sir Wm' Manners (taken out of public use) in *c*.1817,[99] and just a short track remained in 2017, leading to a footpath.

The 9th earl of Dysart and his trustees spent heavily on improvements from the 1880s, employing an estate architect.[100] It is no exaggeration to say that the earl upgraded his inheritance of an estate village into a model village. Bull Row was demolished and replaced in 1886–8 by 18 semi-detached family homes on large plots, including The Crescent (Fig. 3).[101] With three bedrooms, a half-acre garden and an outhouse, these 'little palaces' were praised in 1893 for their design and quality by assistant parliamentary commissioner William Bear.[102] Large stables were built to the east of the village green in *c*.1888, with a stone entrance arch flanked by two Tuscan

Figure 3 *The Crescent, Buckminster.*

96   *London Gaz.*, 22 Apr. 1969, 4210–11.
97   John Rylands Libr., BAG 13/5/2.
98   Lincs. Arch., DIOC/TER BUNDLE/LEICS/BUCKMINSTER/1605.
99   John Rylands Libr., BAG 13/5/2, annotations on rough sketch.
100 *Grantham Jnl*, 21 Apr. 1888; C.N. Wright, *Dir. of Leics.* (1887–8), 368.
101 Date tablet on each house.
102 *Royal Commission on Labour, Third Report (Agricultural Labourer), Reports by W.E. Bear* (Parl. Papers
     1893–4 [C.6894–1]) p. 139; property particulars at http://www.buckminster.co.uk/wp-content/
     uploads/2017/06/Particulars-June-2017-PDF.pdf (accessed 23 Jun. 2017).

columns on each side, a stone pediment, and stone pilasters between each red-brick bay (Fig. 4).[103] Three farms in the centre of the village were also upgraded in this period.[104]

A brick water tower was built by Lord Dysart in 1912,[105] with the water piped from Sewstern.[106] Its size and location suggest it was not intended to be solely for the use of the

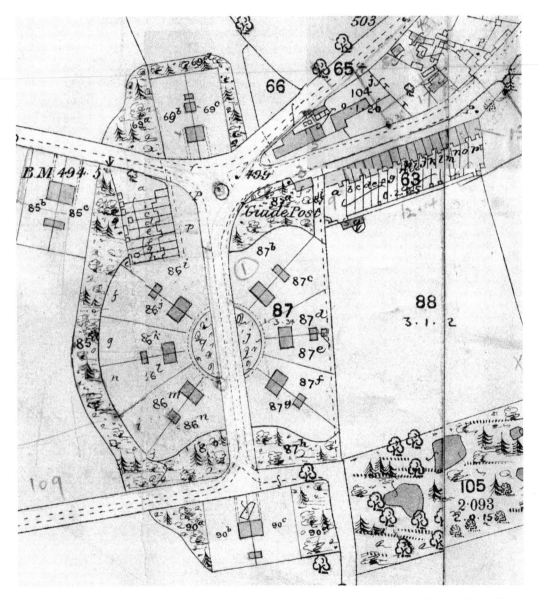

Map 6 *Buckminster village in c.1888, showing the new houses forming The Crescent, and the last of the Bull Row houses immediately prior to demolition.*

103   ROLLR, DE 3736/box 39; *Grantham Jnl*, 21 Apr. 1888; Pevsner, *Leics.*, 117.
104   Below, 50.
105   Date tablet on building.
106   L. Richardson, *Wells and Springs of Leicestershire* (1931), 83.

Hall, although a number of wells and pumps remained in use.[107] This water tower became redundant in the 20th century, when Anglian Water Company built a concrete water tower in the parish (The Ashes), near the junction of Hall Road and Sewstern Lane.

Six houses 'for our own workmen' were built by the estate on Sproxton Road in 1935, and were known as Jubilee Cottages, it being the silver jubilee of the coronation of George V.[108] Lord Dysart was 'anxious … to introduce as far as possible all up to date improvements in cottage building', and showed a close interest in the specifications, objecting to tiled floors for the living rooms as 'a damned rheumaticy [sic] thing to keep your feet on'.[109] He considered Cow Row to be 'a blot on the face of the Earth', but was deterred from demolition by the cost of rebuilding 17 homes in a style and on sufficient land to harmonise with the others.[110] The Crescent and Jubilee Cottages earned plaudits from the Council for the Protection of Rural England in *c*.1945.[111]

Figure 4 *The former stables, with the 1912 water tower in the background. Buckminster's cricket pitch is in the foreground.*

107   These include one which is Grade II listed: NHL, no. 1061283, Water Pump at Stables 30 m. NW of Tollemache Arms, (accessed 20 Apr. 2014).

108   Date tablet on buildings; Surr. HC, K 58/17/37, letter 15 Feb. 1935.

109   Surr. HC, K 58/17/37, letters 12 Feb. 1935, 25 Feb. 1935.

110   Surr. HC, K 58/17/37, letter 1 Feb. 1935.

111   Council for the Protection of Rural England, Leics. Branch, *Save Leicestershire's Countryside* (Leicester, not dated, *c*.1945), 39.

The village's built character has been maintained since the 9th earl's death in 1935 through the careful matching of styles when a terrace of six houses was built on Coston Road in 1948, and the subsequent renovation of older properties in preference to rebuilding.[112] Buckminster Hall shared the fate of many country houses, and was demolished in 1951. Unusually, a replacement house was built in 1965, on a scale more appropriate to the 20th century.[113] Cow Row was renovated, modernised and renamed 'The Row'. The stables, which were used to accommodate Italian, and then German prisoners of war during the Second World War,[114] became a hostel for displaced persons after the war,[115] accommodation for ironstone workers in the 1950s[116], for Kesteven Teacher Training College in the 1960s,[117] and for the rehabilitation of ex-prisoners in the 1970s.[118] Renamed Hanby House, the building was subsequently converted and let as flats. The former estate workshops in the centre of the village became a development of 11 office units in 2012,[119] and the former smithy was converted to offices in 2016.[120]

Sewstern

Sewstern's medieval chapel, present by 1220, was at the west end of the village,[121] and this may have been the heart of the original settlement. A 'green' and a 'west green', both within Sewstern, are recorded in (undated) copies of medieval charters,[122] suggesting two foci had developed, and traders may have established themselves around the junction where Main Street meets Sewstern Lane to provide travellers with board, lodging and overnight grazing for their horses.

The houses are mostly laid out along the two sides of Main Street, many having a long thin paddock of *c*.2–3 r. to the rear (Map 2), although some of the paddocks had been merged in 2017. Similar village plans elsewhere may be the result of late settlement on former arable strips,[123] and a charter of 1416 which transfers a messuage in Sewstern with a garden and one selion in a croft may support this interpretation.[124] That said, the width of the strips varies, and given the range of trade and craft occupations seen in 1381,[125] they may have been deliberately created by Vaudey abbey as lord of the manor and major

---

112 Date tablet on buildings.
113 Below, 38.
114 Inf. from Geoff Dunkley and Roy Rayson, residents of Buckminster in the 1930s and 1940s [2015–17].
115 ROLLR, DE 8655/103.
116 *Leic. Merc.*, 8 Feb. 1955.
117 Memories of M. McWhinnie, 1962–5, http://www.kestevencollege.com/memories.html (accessed 12 Apr. 2016).
118 Letter to all residents from parish council 26 Jun. 1972 (private collection).
119 http://www.buckminster.co.uk/wp-content/uploads/2014/11/Units-9-11-Buckminster-Yard-Particulars-17-10-14-FINAL-VERSION-28.10.14.pdf (accessed 13 Mar. 2015).
120 http://www.buckminster.co.uk/buckminster-blacksmiths-is-new-home-for-architectural-firm/ (accessed 3 Jan. 2017).
121 TNA, C 66/966, m. 11.
122 Rockingham Castle Arch., C1.7.21, ff. 52v, 55.
123 T. Williamson, R. Liddiard and T. Partida, *Champion: The Making and Unmaking of the English Midland Landscape* (Liverpool, 2013), 83–5.
124 ROLLR, DG 40/197.
125 *Poll Taxes 1377–81*, (ed.) Fenwick, I, 600.

landowner in the late medieval period. The paddocks would have complemented, or may have stimulated, commercial activities, and may possibly indicate an attempt by the abbey to establish a town and market near Sewstern Lane.

Sewstern's houses are individual and predominantly built in limestone. The former Red Lion Inn which sits astride the county boundary may be from the late 16th century.[126] Old Manor Farm (Fig. 5), set well back from the road on the north side of Main Street, may be of similar date. It is of coursed limestone, with a stone mullion window of three lights on the ground floor, two more on the first floor, and two-light mullioned windows in both the east and west garrets. It is listed as dating from *c.*1670, with later additions,[127] but two jettons of *c.*1589–1601 were found in a fireplace and in the garden.[128]

The eighteenth century is well represented. A three-storey pair of semi-detached houses on the north side of Main Street (nos 38–40) seems out-of-place in a rural village (Fig. 6). Built in coursed limestone with a slate roof, there are seven bays, the central one with no door or windows, a central chimney stack and a date-stone inscribed: 'A TW

Figure 5 *Old Manor Farm, Sewstern.*

126 Above, 5.
127 NHL, no. 1061285, Old Manor Farmhouse (accessed 4 May 2015).
128 Inf. from Michael Goodacre, former owner [2016].

1752'. The central of the three bays on each side has a door, with two blind windows above, and there are attic windows at each end of the building.[129] The most likely builder was Thomas Watkinson, a wealthy woolcomber, who married Ann Lavidge in 1739. His 'brother', John Mason, was also a woolcomber,[130] and may have shared the house. Watkinson served in all four parish offices between 1724 and 1754, took a parish apprentice in 1745, and died in 1767.[131] The Blue Dog inn, a short distance to its west and also built of limestone in the 18th century, served as both a farmhouse and an inn (also Fig. 6).[132] The name references Lord Huntingtower's 'Blue' political interest,[133] indicating where refreshments were available to those voting for his son during parliamentary elections in the 1820s. A number of other limestone houses along Main Street also appear to be of the 18th century, including several former farmhouses which were built at right angles to the road, probably because of the narrow nature of the plots.

Figure 6 *The Blue Dog and 38–40 Main Street, Sewstern.*

129 NHL, no. 1061284, Pair of Farmhouses, Front Railing and Boundary Wall (accessed 4 May 2015).
130 ROLLR, Wills, 1767.
131 A. Fox (ed.), *Parish Government in a Leicestershire Village: The Buckminster Town Book, 1665–1767 and Constable's Book, 1755–1813* (Leicester, 2015), 30, 33, 40–1, 45–6, 49; ROLLR, Parish registers; PR/T/1767/234.
132 NHL, no. 1360832, The Blue Dog (accessed 4 May 2015).
133 *Stamford Merc.*, 10 Dec. 1824; 24 Oct. 1828.

Holy Trinity church on Back Lane was built in 1842 on an empty plot.[134] Eight or ten houses were built in the village by John Clarke immediately before the First World War.[135] Six houses were built in the 1950s for agricultural workers, and there was also a small amount of private residential building in the late 20th and early 21st centuries. A water tower was erected in Sewstern by Severn Trent Water Authority in 1970, but had been removed by the early 1990s.[136]

Population

There were 31 heads of households in Buckminster in 1086 suggesting a population of 140–150 people.[137] Sewstern was much smaller, with just seven people enumerated in 1086,[138] perhaps equating to 30–35 inhabitants. A period of substantial growth followed, with 178 people across the parish paying the poll tax of 1377,[139] equating to an overall population of about 270, which may have been higher immediately before the Black Death. The 1381 poll tax, the year of the peasants' revolt, lists the villages separately, but the total of just 129 people listed suggests a high level of evasion.[140]

By 1563, the two villages comprised one of the most populous parishes in north-east Leicestershire, with the number of residents exceeded only by Melton Mowbray and by Bottesford with its hamlets.[141] Buckminster was then the larger of the two villages, with 35 households, against 28 in Sewstern, including the three houses to the east of Sewstern Lane.[142] This would suggest village populations of around 160 and 125 respectively, a total little changed from 1377. The 252 communicants recorded within the two villages in 1603, perhaps 375 people, suggests significant population growth over the late 16th century.[143] This was not unusual in north-east Leicestershire, indeed some villages, including Long Clawson and Stapleford, were growing faster in this period.[144] Stagnation apparently followed, with 251 communicants in 1676.[145] This figure may mask different experiences in the two villages. The Hearth Tax recorded 35 houses in Buckminster in 1670, the same as in 1563, and 36 in Sewstern, which was eight more than in 1563.[146] Vicar John Dixon recorded 93 families and 389 souls living in the parish in 1709.[147] Buckminster had 40

---

134 ROLLR, DE 76 Ti/279/1; CERC 16440; below, 97–9.
135 *Grantham Jnl*, 21 May 1913.
136 B. Barton, *Water Towers of Britain* (2003), 118.
137 *Domesday*, 630.
138 *Domesday*, 643.
139 *Poll Taxes 1377–81*, (ed.) Fenwick, I, 485.
140 *Poll Taxes 1377–81*, (ed.) Fenwick, I, 600, 603.
141 Dyer and Palliser (eds), *Diocesan Population Returns*, 214–16.
142 Ibid., 192, 215, 216.
143 A. Whiteman, *The Compton Census of 1676: A Critical Edition* (1986), 339 n., revising the figure in Dyer and Palliser.
144 Dyer and Palliser (eds), *Diocesan Population Returns*, 376–8.
145 Whiteman, *Compton Census*, 339.
146 *VCH Leics*. III, 170.
147 J. Broad (ed.), *Bishop Wake's Summary of Visitation Returns from the Diocese of Lincoln 1705–15* (Oxford, 2012), II, 755.

houses in 1730, when Sewstern was the larger village with 46 homes.[148] In 1790, there were 38 families in Buckminster and 44 in Sewstern.[149]

The national census recorded 262 people in Buckminster in 1801 and 221 in Sewstern. The apparent change in the relative size of the two villages follows the building of Buckminster Hall and Bull Row. Buckminster remained the more populous of the two villages at least until the two civil parishes were merged in 1936, when separate figures ceased to be available. Both villages saw the population peak in 1831, when there were 474 people in Buckminster and 368 in Sewstern, partly due to an influx of Irish labourers employed on a temporary basis by Lord Huntingtower, and the inclusion of *c.*70 Grantham freemen, who moved to Skillington in 1832.[150] The overall trend was then one of decline in Buckminster until the 1880s, and in Sewstern until the early 20th century. In 1931, the last year for which separate figures were recorded, there were 265 people living in Buckminster, and 241 in Sewstern, very similar figures to those seen in 1801. The total of 506 in 1931 remained virtually unchanged in 1951, but the next 20 years saw further decline, to a total population of 357 in 1971.[151] The number of residents then stabilised; in 2011 the total population of the two villages was 356.[152]

148 Nichols, *History*, II, 123.
149 Ibid.
150 Below, 66; *Morning Post*, 31 Oct. 1832.
151 Census.
152 https://neighbourhood.statistics.gov.uk/dissemination/LeadTableView (accessed 17 May 2016).

LANDOWNERSHIP

Buckminster was held by R. FitzWalter in 1086, under the bishop of Lincoln, and Sewstern was held by William Lovet. Over the next 300 years, both manors and much of the land in the parish were acquired by two religious houses: Buckminster manor was given to Kirby Bellars chantry chapel (later priory) in 1317, and by 1323 Vaudey abbey (Lincs.) held Sewstern manor and over 1,000 a. of land in the parish. Vaudey abbey let Sewstern manor and its land in the parish to Kirby Bellars chapel in 1323, and from then both manors were administered as a single holding. Croxton abbey, the Knights Templar, Knights Hospitaller and Burton Lazars hospital also held modest quantities of land in the parish. There were no other property holders of significance in the Middle Ages.

Some small land sales created several minor freeholders following the dissolution of the monasteries, but the combined manor and most of the land remained with the crown until 1590. A number of short-term owners followed, before Edward Hartopp purchased the combined manor in 1615. It remained with the Hartopp family until 1763, when the manor was sold to Lord William Manners, the second son of the 2nd duke of Rutland. He and his heirs gradually purchased further land and properties in the parish. In 2017, all the domestic and commercial properties and farmland in Buckminster, and some properties and significant farmland in Sewstern, were owned by the Tollemache family, descendants of Lord William Manners.

Buckminster Manor to 1323

Buckminster was held by Healfdene in 1066, but by 1086 the manor was in the hands of the bishop of Lincoln and held by R. FitzWalter under the bishop.[1] Only the bishop, as overlord, was named in 1130.[2] Adam de Bugmenistre was patron of the church and probably lord of the manor in 1220,[3] holding under a mesne lord, who held from the bishop. The next recorded lord was Simon de Bokmynystre, who held the manor of David de Fletewyk by homage and foreign service, and died in 1298.[4] The manor was then worth £14 7s. 5d. annually, and comprised the manor house, 8½ virgates (408 a.)

1   Domesday, 630. R. FitzWalter cannot be identified: K.S.B. Keats-Rohan, Domesday People: A Prosopography of persons occurring in English Documents 1066–1166, I (Woodbridge, 1999); K.S.B. Keats-Rohan, Domesday Descendants: A Prosopography of persons occurring in English Documents 1066–1166, II (Woodbridge, 2002).
2   C.F. Slade, The Leicestershire Survey, c.A.D. 1130 (Leicester, 1956), 22.
3   W.P.W. Phillimore (ed.), Rotuli Hugonis de Welles, II (Lincoln: Lincoln Rec. Soc., VI, 1913), 289.
4   Cal. Inq. p.m. III, 350. Inquisitions following the deaths of David de Fletewyk and his son and heir, also David, do not mention Buckminster: Cal. Inq. p.m. III, 210; V, 177.

of demesne land valued at £5 8s., land of customary tenants worth £6 8s. annually, and annual rents of £2 7s. 1d. from free tenants and 4s. 4d. from cottars.[5] Simon's son William, a minor in 1298, received his lands in 1306.[6] In 1308, he brought a case against David de Fletewyk for making waste and destruction of houses and lands.[7] David claimed in turn against Ralph, a parson who held two parts of a messuage and 11 bovates of land during William's minority, but Ralph pleaded that he was a clerk with no lay fee, giving the court no authority to impose a monetary order against him.[8] William was probably the Sir William de Bokmonstre listed within a parliamentary roll of c.1312, whose arms match those displayed in Buckminster church in the 17th century.[9]

William de Bukminster sold the manor in 1316 to Roger Beler of Kirby Bellars, and Roger's wife Alice,[10] but may have continued to live in the manor house as a tenant, since a William de Bokeminster is recorded in the village in 1327.[11] In 1317, Beler sought release from David, son of David de Fletewyk, from all services due to the bishop of Lincoln,[12] and gave the manor to the warden of his chantry chapel in Kirby Bellars, 13 miles west of Buckminster.[13] In 1319, the manor became part of the foundation grant for a new college of chaplains at Kirby Bellars (which became Kirby Bellars priory).[14]

Sewstern Manor to 1323

The manor of Sewstern was held by William Lovet in 1086,[15] and comprised five carucates of land, or c.960 a. if the carucate was the same size in both villages.[16] This is almost certainly the five carucates in 'Buckminster and in Sewstern' held in 1130 by William Meschin,[17] the brother of Ranulf, earl of Chester.[18] William Meschin died before 1135, and his son Ranulf died, childless, before 1140. William's daughter Alice became co-heir, and appears to have received all the Sewstern land. This passed in due course

5 TNA, C 134/84/3.
6 *Cal. Close*, 1302–7, 414.
7 TNA, CP 40/170, m. 140d. See http://aalt.law.uh.edu/E2/CP40no170/bCP40no170dorses/IMG_0886. htm) (accessed 23 Mar. 2016).
8 TNA, CP 40/187, m. 247d. See http://aalt.law.uh.edu/E2/CP40no187/bCP40no187dorses/IMG_0496. htm (accessed 23 Mar. 2016).
9 Burton, 57; http://aspilogia.com/N-Parliamentary_Roll/N-0592-0701.html (accessed 13 Feb. 2017).
10 TNA, CP 25/1/124/50, no. 130. See http://www.medievalgenealogy.org.uk/fines/abstracts/ CP_25_1_124_50.shtml#130 (accessed 8 Mar. 2016).
11 W.G.D. Fletcher, 'The earliest Leicestershire lay subsidy roll, 1327', *Assoc. Archit. Soc. Rep. & Papers*, 19 (1887–8), 218.
12 TNA, CP 40/221, m. 236. See http://aalt.law.uh.edu/E2/CP40no221/aCP40no221fronts/IMG_0478.htm (accessed 17 Jul. 2016).
13 *Cal. Pat.* 1317–21, 135; TNA, C 143/134/14; E 326/8773.
14 *Cal. Pat.* 1317–21, 393; TNA, CP 25/1/124/52, no. 177. See http://www.medievalgenealogy.org.uk/fines/ abstracts/CP_25_1_124_52.shtml#177 (accessed 8 Mar. 2016). The grant to the collegiate foundation (Lincs. Arch., REG. III, ff. 340–4) was published in A. Hamilton Thompson, 'The chapel of St Peter at Kirkby-upon-Wreake (Kirby Bellars)', *Trans LAHS*, 16 (1929–31), 166–91.
15 *Domesday*, 643.
16 TNA, C 134/84/3.
17 Slade, *Leicestershire Survey*, 22.
18 Keats-Rohan, *Domesday Descendants* II, 1039.

to her daughter and co-heir Cicely, who married William le Gros, count of Aumale (d. 1179).[19] He founded the Cistercian abbey of *Valle Dei*, or Vaudey (Lincs.) in 1147,[20] and probably let some of his land in Sewstern to the abbey, which built a grange here by 1227.[21]

Sewstern manor and the land presumably passed to William and Cicely's daughter and co-heir Hawise, whose second husband was William de Forz (d. 1195). Their son William died in 1241. His son, William de Forz, or de Fortibus, held five carucates in Sewstern in chief from the king by knight service at his death in 1260. Thomas de Seustern held these five carucates under him for 10s. yearly, but retained only three bovates (*c*.72 a.) in hand. Of the remainder, Vaudey abbey held 27 bovates (*c*.648 a.) of Thomas for 25s. 3d. annually, the Knights Templar held two virgates of him in frankalmoign; two people (Simon Russel and Robert Gilbert) each held one virgate of Thomas, and two others each held one bovate. Three of these last four tenants paid a total annual rent of 1s. 9d., but the fourth rent was not recorded.[22]

The surviving children of William de Fortibus (d. 1260) were minors at his death, and both his sons died before they came of age. His only daughter Aveline became the sole heiress of a substantial estate, including land in several counties. She married Edmund Crouchback, earl of Lancaster and Leicester, the second son of Henry III. Aveline came of age in 1273, but died childless in 1274.[23] Twelve claimants to her estate emerged: eleven descendants of the siblings of William le Gros or his wife Cicely, and one, John de Eston, who claimed descent from Anice, an otherwise unrecorded daughter of William le Gros and Cicely. De Eston's possibly fanciful pedigree was accepted by the jurors. He was awarded the lands, which he swiftly quitclaimed to Edward I in exchange for a modest annuity.[24]

Vaudey abbey continued to increase its landholding in the parish. A cartulary, probably begun in the late 14th century, but including copies of earlier charters, and continuing to 1414, records 49 separate, undated, grants of land in favour of Vaudey. These total over 26 bovates (*c*.624 a.) in Sewstern and 20 bovates (*c*.480 a.) in 'Buckminster and Sewstern'. At least 33 of these grants were gifts.[25] Other known grants to Vaudey include a messuage and five bovates from William and Constance de Asgerhagh in 1305–6,[26] and five bovates from Thomas, son of William le Loverd in 1313.[27] Vaudey abbey also acquired Sewstern manor at an unknown date. In 1323, facing financial difficulties, the abbot let the manor and grange of Sewstern, its courts, lands

19   B. English, *The Lords of Holderness, 1086–1260: a study in feudal society* (Oxford, 1979), 17.
20   *VCH Lincs.* II, 143; *ODNB*, s.v. William le Gros, count of Aumale and earl of York (*c*.1110–79), magnate (accessed 8 Nov. 2016).
21   *Cal. Chart.*, 1226–57, 3.
22   *Cal. Inq. p.m.* IV, 349.
23   *ODNB*, s.v. 'Forz, Isabella de, suo jure countess of Devon, and countess of Aumale (1237–93)' (accessed 18 May 2016); 'Edmund, first earl of Lancaster and first earl of Leicester (1245–96)' (accessed 27 Dec. 2016).
24   English, *Lords of Holderness*, 53–4; A. Beanlands, 'The claim of John de Eston', *Miscellanea*, Thoresby Soc., 24 (1919), 227–44.
25   Rockingham Castle Arch., C1.7.21; G.R.C. Davis, *Medieval Cartularies of Great Britain: A Short Catalogue* (1958), 58.
26   *Cal. Inq. p.m. sive Esc.*, I, 212.
27   *Cal. Pat.* 1313–17, 13; TNA, C 143/4/17. Nichols also records five bovates and a messuage from Richard de Lovere, also known as Richard de Asterhaigh: Nichols, *History*, II, 122.

and services of its tenants, to the collegiate chapel at Kirby Bellars, accepting immediately 'a certain sum of money' in commutation of 80-years' future rent, with an annual rent of £16 applying from the end of that term.[28]

Buckminster and Sewstern Manors, 1323–1536

When Kirby Bellars chapel became an Augustinian priory in 1359, its holding of the manor and lands at Sewstern was described as being of demise of the abbot of Vaudey 'for ever'.[29] By 1359 it had also acquired from the Hospitallers 'at fee farm forever' the rents and services of the 'sometime tenants of the Templars' in Sewstern.[30] This holding originally comprised half a carucate plus 5 a. of land and a toft in Sewstern from Richard de Seuesterne, and half a bovate from William de Raimes, both given to the Templars before 1185.[31] It was recorded as two virgates in 1287, held in frankalmoign.[32] The Templars received 5s. 7½d. annual rent for this holding when their lands were seized by the crown in 1308.[33] The order was dissolved in 1312, and their lands transferred to the Knights Hospitaller in c.1314. They had leased the land to Kirby Bellars chapel by 1338, when an extent of the Hospitallers' lands failed to record any land or rents in Buckminster or Sewstern.[34] Between 1345 and 1415, Kirby Bellars priory acquired a further 256 a. of land, 10 a. of meadow, four messuages and a toft in the parish.[35] By 1535, and probably from a much earlier date, the prior was also collecting rents on behalf of the bishop of Lincoln.[36]

In 1532 the priory agreed a lease for 60 years to Thomas Bagott of a 'tenantry in the town of Buckminster called the lordship' for 43s. 4d. annually, with 'stewardship of the towns of Buckminster and Sewstern' for life, and conditions relating to repairs, rebuilding in the case of fire and providing food twice yearly for the keeper of the manor courts. The lease also included two other pieces of land for a further 13s. 4d. annually.[37] The unusual wording caused later confusion, but this appears to be a 60-year lease of the manor house and at least part of the demesne land, with a farm (lease) of the manor and its rents, but not its courts, for life.

---

28   *VCH Lincs.* II, 143; *Cal. Pat.* 1321–4, 356.
29   Hamilton Thompson, 'Chapel', 209–10.
30   Ibid., 209.
31   B.A. Lees (ed.), *Records of the Templars in England in the Twelfth Century: The Inquest of 1185* (1935), 113.
32   *Cal. Inq. p.m.* IV, 349.
33   TNA, E 358/19, rots 27(2), 40. I am very grateful to Prof. Helen Nicolson for this information.
34   L.B. Larking (ed.), *The Knights Hospitallers in England being the Report of Prior Philip de Thame to the Grand Master Elyan de Villanova for AD 1338* (1857).
35   *Cal. Pat.* 1391–6, 140–1; TNA, C 143/421/29, E 326/3236; E 326/3241; E 326/573; E 326/6577; Rockingham Castle, C1.7.21, ff. 14v–15, 46v–47, 50.
36   *Valor Eccl.* IV, 149.
37   TNA, SC 6/HenVIII/1825; C 78/39/7.

The Manors from 1536

1536–90

Kirby Bellars priory and Vaudey abbey were both dissolved in 1536,[38] and the manors and their land passed to the crown, which also treated the two manors as a single entity. Purchasers may have been deterred by the bishop of Lincoln's overlordship of Buckminster manor. In 1547, the crown agreed an exchange of manors and lands with the bishop, including the manor of 'Sewstern' (presumably the manor termed 'Buckminster' in other records).[39] This enabled the crown to sell both manors together, free of any overlordship, but no sale was achieved until 1590, perhaps partly because of the lease which was in place until 1592.[40]

Thomas Bagott (the tenant of the 'lordship') died in 1541.[41] Henry Digby, who had been granted a lease of Buckminster rectory in 1543,[42] was asked by crown officials by 1546 if he would 'take all the town of Bukmynster and Sewystern in farm', presumably referring to the (combined) manor and remaining demesne land. He replied that in view of 'its ruinous state', he would want an allowance to be made for repairs, which would cost over £40.[43] By 1549, Digby had acquired 620 a. in the parish (see below), but it appears that no agreement was reached in respect of the manor, as no lease was mentioned when this was sold by the crown in 1590.

By 1539, Bagott had assigned the remaining term in his 60-year lease of 'the lordship' (the manor house and alienated demesne land) to Robert Lyvesey.[44] The freeholds of the land and property within this lease, formerly owned by Kirby Bellars priory, were granted by the crown to Thomas Manners, 1st earl of Rutland, in 1541, who sold them to Henry Allen.[45] Henry's son and heir, also Henry, granted a lease to Richard Allen in c.1562, who tried to evict Lyvesey, claiming Lyvesey had allowed the hall, brewhouse and kilne house to become ruinous, in breach of his covenants. Lyvesey, who by then also held a 21-year crown lease of land with an annual rent of £7 11s. 4d., successfully claimed he had repaired and rebuilt the property.[46] It is not clear whether he or his heirs remained in possession until 1592.

An inquisition held on the death of Henry Allen (I) in 1549 found that he held only a capital messuage (manor house), one close and 90 a. of arable, meadow and pasture in Buckminster, almost certainly the freehold of the 'lordship' holding occupied by Lyvesey.[47] Shortly before his death, Allen had also purchased 620 a. of arable, meadow,

---

38   *VCH Leics.* II, 26; *VCH Lincs.* II, 144.
39   *Cal. Pat. Edw. VI,* I, 153–4.
40   *Cal. Pat. 32* Eliz. I, 1589–90 (L&I Soc. vol. 301), 155.
41   G. Wrottesley, 'A history of the Bagot family *Collections for a History of Staffordshire* (William Salt Archaeological Section, n.s. 11, 1908), 71.
42   *L&P Hen. VIII,* XVIII (1), 556.
43   *L&P Hen. VIII,* XXI (2), 125.
44   TNA, C 78/39/7.
45   *L&P Hen. VIII,* XVI, 457; TNA, C 78/39, m. 13.
46   TNA, C 66/966, mm. 11–12, C 78/39/7; C 3/110/4.
47   TNA, WARD 7/5/57.

pasture, woodland and properties in Buckminster and Sewstern from Henry Digby
for 100 marks (£66 13s. 4d.), although this purchase was not registered by the courts
until after he died, hence its omission from the inquest findings. The transaction was
warranted by Henry Manners, 2nd earl of Rutland.[48] The earl may have been a previous
owner; his father Thomas, the 1st earl, had sold land in Buckminster and Sewstern
formerly belonging to Croxton abbey to Digby in 1540, and may also have acquired other
former monastic land in the parish.[49] Although the acreage held by Croxton abbey was
not recorded at the time of the sale, other records suggest this was only about 5 a.[50]

1590–1763

Elizabeth I sold the manor of Buckminster and Sewstern in 1590 to Henry Best (a
scrivener) and Francis Goston, both of London, including lands within 13 crown leases,
of unspecified acreage, with many under-tenants.[51]

The same year Henry (II), Bridget and Richard Allen sold 720 a. arable, meadow,
pasture, moor, furze and heath in Buckminster and Sewstern to John and Anne Allen for
£80.[52] This was almost certainly the 620 a. Henry Allen (I) had purchased from Digby,
together with the 'lordship' house and land purchased from Thomas Manners, earl of
Rutland. The holding was soon broken up, with the sale of 260 a. to George Gylson in
1593, an unspecified amount of land to Alexander Glover in 1593, and three virgates
(144 a.), 4 a. and a close to Thomas and William Wensley in 1594.[53] In 1596, Allen
received licence to sell to Thomas and Henry Cave the 'manor', 'courts', 'lordship', and
other land, but the mention of a manor and its courts may stem from confusion over
the meaning of the Allen's ownership of the 'tenantry known as the lordship', as he didn't
hold the manor.[54] The sale itself only mentioned four properties and 80 a. of arable,
meadow, pasture, furze and heath.[55]

The manor was sold by Best and Goston at an unknown date, and in 1612 was held
by Sir William and Elisabeth Smythe. They sold it that year, with nine houses, a windmill
and 1,000 a. of arable, meadow, pasture, furze and heath, to Thomas's son Alexander
Cave for £300.[56] Alexander sold the manor with 800 a. of arable, meadow, pasture, furze
and heath in 1615 to Edward Hartopp for £300.[57]

Edward Hartopp was probably resident in the parish: he had children baptised in
Buckminster church in 1611, 1613 and 1615, and signed a document from Sewstern in
1637.[58] He was created baronet in 1619, and made other smaller purchases of land in the

---

48   *Cal. Pat.* Edw. VI, I, 361; TNA, CP 25/2/60/459/2/3EdwVIHil, rot. 29–29d.
49   Lincs. Arch., 1PG/1/70.
50   Below, 32.
51   *Cal. Pat.* 32 Eliz. I, 1589–90 (L&I Soc. vol. 301), 155; TNA, C 66/1351, mm. 5–9.
52   TNA, CP 25/2/166/2670/32/33ElizIMich, rot. 8.
53   TNA, CP 25/2/166/2681/35/36ElizIMich, rot. 18–18d; C 66/1589, mm. 5–6; *Cal. Pat.* 44 Eliz. I, 1601–2
      (L&I Soc. vol. 349), 187.
54   TNA, C 66/1464, mm. 22–23.
55   TNA, CP 25/2/166/2694/39ElizIEaster, rot. 19; Farnham I, 232.
56   TNA, CP 25/2/314/10JasIEaster, rot. 18.
57   Farnham I, 233; the bundle is missing at TNA. Farnham also names Thomas Cave as a party, but he had
      died in 1609: *Hist. Parl. Commons* 1558–1603, I, 565.
58   Parish registers; *Cal. SP Dom.* XI, 418.

parish, for example in 1634 and 1635.[59] He died in 1654, having settled the manor and his Buckminster land on his son, also Edward, and heirs.[60] His widow Mary mentioned houses in both Buckminster and Sewstern in a letter of *c*.1654 to her brother Sir John Dryden discussing her dower.[61] Shortly before his death in 1657, Sir Edward (II) resettled the estate on his son John and male heirs.[62] Sir John Hartopp inherited, and on his death in 1722 the manor and lands passed to his son, also named John.[63] The latter died in 1762, and his will directed that all his debts, cash legacies, and the bequests detailed in a separate letter of wishes were to be paid out of his manor of Buckminster and Sewstern, which was therefore sold.[64]

From 1763

The manor was purchased in 1763 by Lord William Manners, the second son of the 2nd duke of Rutland.[65] Lord William (d. 1772) settled the manor and his other lands in the parish on his eldest (illegitimate) son John, and John's male heirs.[66] John married Lady Louisa Talmash, the eldest daughter of the 4th earl of Dysart (a Scottish peerage).[67] Through the purchase of further land and properties, by 1789 his total landholdings in Buckminster and Sewstern had increased to 884 a. 2 r. 11p.[68] When he died in 1792, his personal property was 'worth £400,000 exclusive of his family estate, all of which he is supposed to have acquired by play'.[69] Although a substantial acreage, the villages still 'belong[ed] in a great measure to the freeholders; of whom there are about 30 in each village'.[70] John's eldest son William inherited. He decided to make Buckminster his home, and employed Humphry Repton for advice on a new mansion.[71]

William Manners was created a baronet in 1793.[72] In 1821, his mother became the 7th countess of Dysart in her own right, on the death of her brother Wilbraham. William became the heir to the earldom, taking the courtesy title Lord Huntingtower, and changing his surname by royal licence to Talmash (later Tollemache).[73] He made regular purchases of land in Buckminster and Sewstern, especially in the depressed years following the end of the Napoleonic Wars in 1815, and by 1829 owned 1,609 a. within the parish.[74] He died in 1833. His eldest son Lionel inherited, taking the title Lord

59   G.E. Cokayne, *Complete Baronetage*, I (Exeter, 1900–09), 131–2; TNA, CP 25/2/447/10ChasITrin, rot. 4–4d; CP 25/2/447/10ChasIHil, rot. 7.
60   TNA, PROB 11/250/81.
61   Northants. RO, 165-D (CA) 923, f. 19.
62   Cokayne, *Complete Baronetage*, I, 131–2; ROLLR, 42D31/119.
63   Cokayne, *Complete Baronetage*, I, 131–2.
64   TNA, PROB 11/873/5, f. 11.
65   Lincs. Arch., BA 1189/2/23.
66   TNA, PROB 11/977/309.
67   *Complete Peerage*, IV, 564.
68   Lincs. Arch., BA 1189/2/23.
69   *Stamford Merc.*, 4 Jun. 1772.
70   Nichols, *Additional*, 1021.
71   Below, 35–6.
72   Cokayne, *Complete Baronetage*, V, 284.
73   *London Gaz.*, 14 Apr. 1821, 838.
74   ROLLR, QS 62/61; Buckminster Estate Arch., Lordships map.

Huntingtower until 1840, when he became the 8th earl of Dysart, on his grandmother's death.[75] With other houses available to him, the 8th earl chose not to live in Buckminster, although he maintained a close interest in how the land was farmed, and continued to acquire land in the parish, at least for the first few years.[76] Those agreeing to sell their property to him were pointedly advised in 1838 that their rent as tenants would reflect the sum they had received.[77] By 1841, he owned 2,019 a. in the parish (about two-thirds of the land).[78]

The 8th earl died in 1878.[79] In 1873, his estate had included 27,190 a. in Leicestershire, Lincolnshire, Surrey and Rutland.[80] His son, William, Lord Huntingtower, had been declared bankrupt in 1842, and died in 1872,[81] when his creditors under the bankruptcy remained unpaid (hearings continued until 1887).[82] In order to protect the estate from claims by his late son's creditors, the 8th earl's will placed the manors, lands and properties in trust for a period of 21 years from his (the 8th earl's) death, then passing to his grandson William (the 9th earl) for life, and thence to the 9th earl's male heirs.[83] The 9th earl married Cecilia Newton in 1885,[84] but they separated and had no children. Land acquisition continued, but at a slower pace. By 1910, Lord Dysart owned 2,246 a. across Buckminster and Sewstern, including 1,571 a. of land and all but eight houses in Buckminster.[85] In 1934 he conveyed his interest in his Leicestershire, Lincolnshire and Surrey estates to a company established for that purpose, 'Buckminster Estates'.[86]

The beneficial owners of the estate between 1935 and 1963 were the holders of the baronetcy, which passed from Lord Dysart to his second cousin Lyonel Tollemache, 4th baronet. (The Scottish peerage passed to Lord Dysart's niece Wynefryde Greaves.)[87] Sir Lyonel died in 1952, and was succeeded by his son Sir (Cecil) Lyonel.[88] The Buckminster Estates company was dissolved in 1963, with the assets transferred to family trusts.[89] When the 5th baronet died in 1969, the baronetcy and interest in the manor and estate passed to his 72-year old brother, Major-General Humphry Tollemache.[90] Sir Humphry's eldest son Lyonel moved into Buckminster Park when the new hall was built in 1965,[91] and became the 7th baronet on the death of his father in 1990.[92] In 2008, Sir Lyonel and

75   *Complete Peerage*, IV, 566.
76   *Grantham Jnl*, 5 Oct. 1878; Buckminster Estate Arch., for example, item 4, letters 17 Jun. 1835, 17 Apr. 1838.
77   Buckminster Estate Arch., item 8, letter 9 Mar. 1838.
78   ROLLR, Ti/53/1; Ti/279/11.
79   Principal Probate Registry, COW57116g.
80   *Return of Owners of Land in England and Wales* (Parl. Papers 1874 [C.1097] lxxii), pp. Lincs. 32, Leics. 10, Rutl. 2, Surr. 9).
81   *London Gaz.*, 25 Oct. 1842, 2957; *Complete Peerage*, IV, 566.
82   *London Gaz.*, 18 Mar. 1887, 1649.
83   Principal Probate Registry, COW57116g.
84   *Complete Peerage*, IV, 567.
85   ROLLR, DE 2072/111.
86   Surr. HC, K 58/13/182; TNA, 31/39572/288593.
87   *The Times*, 23 Nov. 1935, 16.
88   Ibid., 5 Mar. 1952, 6.
89   *London Gaz.*, 1 Mar. 1963, 194; TNA, 31/39572/288593.
90   *The Times*, 2 Apr. 1969, 12.
91   Inf. from Sir Lyonel Tollemache [2015].
92   *The Times*, 3 Apr. 1990, 16.

his wife moved to the Old Vicarage in Buckminster, where they continued to live in 2017, and their son Richard moved into Buckminster Park with his wife and children. In 2017, the Tollemache family owned all the land, residential and commercial properties in Buckminster, but there were other freeholders in Sewstern.[93]

Minor Estates in the Middle Ages

The Land of Robert de Ferrers

There were three capital holdings in Buckminster and Sewstern in 1130, the third being half a carucate held by Robert de Ferrers, 1st earl of Derby (d. 1139).[94] Some of the de Ferrers lands were surrendered to the crown in 1222.[95] If the Sewstern land had been retained, it would have passed in due course to Robert de Ferrers, 6th earl of Derby. The 6th earl's lands were forfeited to the crown in 1266 for his part in an unsuccessful rebellion by disinherited Montfortians, and were granted to Edmund Crouchback, son of Henry III.[96] Edmund became earl of Lancaster, and married Aveline in 1269, who inherited the de Forz manor and lands in Sewstern[97]. At Edmund's death in 1296, he held 1/20 of a knight's fee in Sewstern,[98] which equated to about half a carucate.[99] This was presumably the land that de Ferrers had held in 1130, as Aveline had died childless, and her lands had been acquired by Edward I.[100] This landholding cannot be traced in later records. As an insignificant part of the Duchy of Lancaster estates, it may have been sold.

Other Religious Estates

Mauger de Sewstern, his daughter Alice, her husband Simon Russel, and Simon's son, also Simon, gave 4 a. and 16 selions of land with meadow in 'Sewstern and Buckminster' to Croxton abbey, at an unknown date.[101] The abbey recorded receipt of 3s. 4d. rent from the Sewstern land in 1501, and 7s. 4d. from 'Buckminster' land in 1520.[102] After the abbey surrendered in 1538,[103] Henry VIII initially promised its lands to Thomas Legh, but then gave them to Thomas Manners, 1st earl of Rutland, in 1539.[104] The following

---

93   Inf. from Sir Lyonel and Richard Tollemache [2015].
94   Slade, *Leicestershire Survey*, 22.
95   *ODNB*, s.v. 'Ferrers, Robert de, sixth earl of Derby' (accessed 5 Mar. 2016).
96   Ibid.
97   Above, 26.
98   *Cal. Inq. p.m.* III, 297.
99   The knight's fee was not a fixed amount of land, but in Holywell (Castle Bytham parish, Lincs., nine miles from Buckminster) in 1287 a fee was 8 carucates: *Cal. Inq. p.m.* IV, 350.
100 Above, 26.
101 Belvoir Castle Manuscripts, Add. MS 70, f. 23.
102 Belvoir Castle Manuscripts, Croxton rentals 1 and 3.
103 *VCH Leics.* II, 30.
104 *L&P Hen. VIII*, XIV (2), 74.

year the earl sold his lands in Buckminster and Sewstern to Henry Digby of Tickencote (Rutl.).[105] Digby sold his land to Henry Allen in 1549, as described above.

The hospital of Burton Lazars held land in Sewstern worth 11s. annually in 1535.[106] The figure suggests a modest landholding, but it contributed to the scale of change seen when the religious houses were dissolved. Some of these lands were given by Mary I to her restored religious houses of the Knights Hospitaller and the Hospital of the Savoy.[107] These grants were reversed by Elizabeth I in 1558, and the lands returned to the crown. This holding cannot be identified after that date.

Rectory Estate

The rectory was held by Kirby Bellars Priory from 1363, and let for 10 years to Thomas Bagott in 1534 for £12 annually.[108] After the dissolution, a series of leases were granted by the crown between 1543 and 1589.[109] The last of these (for 21 years) specified that Ralph Probie, Thomas Beverley, Thomas Fludd and Anthony Barker were to repair and maintain the chancel of the church.[110] In 1599 the rectory was sold with the advowson to John Flynt and William Jenkinson of Hardwick (Derb.).[111] They appear to have sold it to the Cavendish family (later earls and dukes of Devonshire), and it was in the hands of the 3rd earl of Devonshire in 1683.[112] It remained with his descendants until 1731, when it was sold by William Cavendish, 3rd duke of Devonshire, to Lord William Manners.[113] The great tithes for Buckminster and Sewstern were commuted in 1842, with annual payments agreed of £390 and £300, respectively.[114]

Vaudey Abbey Grange

Limited excavation in 1967, ahead of quarrying, of a site almost midway between the two villages, to the west of the road linking them and almost on the boundary of the two townships, uncovered the foundations of two buildings, a well and 16.6 lb (7.5 kg) of medieval pottery, largely from the 11th to 14th centuries.[115] This is believed to be Vaudey abbey's grange, and is consistent with documentary evidence that it was built by 1227, and with the assumption that it went out of use as a residence when Vaudey leased the manor and their land to Kirby Bellars chapel in 1323.

105 Lincs. Arch., 1PG/1/70.
106 *Valor Eccl.* IV, 152–3.
107 *Cal. Pat.* 1555–7, 544; *Cal. Pat.* 1557–8, 315–16, 318.
108 TNA, SC 6/HenVIII/7311, m. 8d.; *Valor Eccl.* IV, 149.
109 *Cal. Pat.* 1560–63, 238; *L&P Hen. VIII*, XVIII (1), 556; *Cal. Pat.* 1563–66, 88; *Cal. Pat.* 1578–80, 196.
110 TNA, C 66/1333, mm. 38, 41.
111 *Cal. Pat.* 41 Eliz. I, 1598–99 (L&I Soc. vol. 328), 26–8.
112 ROLLR, 17D 47/1.
113 Surr. HC, K58/15/1.
114 ROLLR, Ti/53/1; Ti/279/1.
115 D. Rudkin, 'The excavation of an early medieval site at Buckminster, Leicestershire', *Trans LAHS*, 47 (1971–2), 1–13; Leics. and Rutl. HER, MLE 3466.

Other Freeholders after 1536

The other landholdings of the former religious houses were let by the crown, mostly in small parcels for terms of 21 years, and eventually sold in 17 separate parcels of land and properties. The most significant sales, other than those already mentioned, were the sale of the rents and reversions contained in six leases of more than three virgates of land (144 a.) to John Duddeley and John Ayscough in 1576, and the sale of over 15 bovates (360 a.) in 1577 to John Fortescue and John Walker, let to six people.[116] Freeholders by the early 17th century included James Brigg (d. 1605) with 90 a.,[117] William Coye (d. 1606) with 137 a.,[118] Roger Jorden (d. 1608) with *c.*108 a.,[119] Arthur and Thomas Storer with 135 a. in 1617,[120] Thomas Glover (d. 1628) with 130 a.,[121] and Francis Forman (d. 1634) with 140 a.[122] These lands were gradually acquired by the manorial lord, mostly over the late 18th and early 19th centuries. The last owners of any significant acreage in Buckminster were the Marshall family. Thomas Marshall paid almost one-fifteenth of the land tax in 1826, suggesting he owned *c.*200 a.[123] By 1840, Arthur, John, John junior and William Marshall owned 135 a. between them in Buckminster, and a further 75 a. in Sewstern.[124]

Buckminster Park

Buckminster Park is an area of modern parkland in the extreme north-east of the parish, where Buckminster Hall was built in *c.*1797. It is also the name of the successor house to the Hall, built in 1965. There is no evidence of a medieval hunting park in Buckminster, and none was listed by Burton.[125]

Origins

Thomas Bagott's lease of 'the lordship' in 1532 appears to have included a manor house. This was a substantial building in 1562, when the hall, brewhouse and kilne house had 'recently' been rebuilt, but its location is not known.[126] The parkland probably has its origins in two other pieces of land included in the 1532 lease, known as Edgecourte or Hedgecroft, and Dallockover or Dallockburne, both 'on the north side of the said lordship', which it was agreed Bagott could inclose.[127] Perhaps totalling 90 a., these may

---

116 TNA, C 66/1148, mm. 22–23, C 66/1155, mm. 20–22.
117 Farnham I, 232, citing TNA, C 142/287/12.
118 Ibid., 232–3, citing TNA, C 142/299/160.
119 Ibid., 233, citing TNA, C 142/301/21.
120 Ibid., 233, citing TNA, C 142/360/44.
121 Ibid., 233–4, citing TNA, C 142/452/17.
122 Ibid., 234, citing TNA, C 142/506/152.
123 ROLLR, QS 62/61.
124 ROLLR, Ti 53/1; Ti 279/1.
125 Burton, 6.
126 TNA, C 78/39/7.
127 TNA, SC 6/HenVIII/1824; C 78/39/7.

have been intended to provide a parkland setting for the medieval manor house.[128] By 1607, the 'ground about the house' contained 120 a.[129] The earliest mention of 'Buckminster Park' by name is in a letter of *c.*1654 from Mary, widow of Sir Edward Hartopp (d. 1654), to her brother Sir John Dryden querying which property would be included in her dower.[130]

The Mansion of 1797

The 'Park' owned and occupied by John Manners in 1789 contained 54 a., but that may exclude neighbouring land owned by him and let for pasture.[131] A Renaissance-style gateway, perhaps of the late 16th or early 17th century, stood in 1790, but the manor house was 'in ruins, and in part converted to a farm-house'.[132] This was then a two-storey stone house with mullioned windows, described as 'part of the old mansion'.[133]

Sir William Manners commissioned Humphry Repton in 1793 to propose a site for a new mansion and plans for landscaping the grounds. Samuel Saxon, a former pupil of Sir William Chambers, was chosen to design the property.[134] The Palladian-style house was probably completed in 1797.[135] Built in ashlar, it had two flanking wings: kitchen and servants' quarters were to the north, and stables (later converted to music and billiards

Figure 7 *Buckminster Hall in 1886, viewed from the east.*

128 TNA, WARD 7/5/57.
129 TNA, E 178/4010.
130 Northants. RO, 165-D (CA) 923, f. 19.
131 Lincs. Arch., BRA 1189/2/23.
132 Nichols, *Additional*, 1021.
133 Nichols, *History*, II, engraving between 122–3.
134 Buckminster Estate Arch., item 7; Pevsner, *Leics.*, 117n.
135 *Observer*, 10 Sept. 1797.

rooms) to the south (Fig. 7).[136] The staircase hall was similar to those in Chambers' London houses.[137]

Lord Dysart employed architect Halsey Ricardo in 1881 to 'enhance the comfort' of the house, improve the garden and generally render 'the building more worthy of its fine site'.[138] Ricardo found that 'the house was in a far worse state than could be ascertained at a first inspection'.[139] The building required underpinning, there was extensive dry rot in the floors and ceiling joists, and four ceilings were 'rotten and dangerous'.[140] After resolving these issues, he turned his attention to the agreed improvements, installing heating, new sanitary ware, and lavish decoration in keeping with the period of the house. In the dining room, this included wall panelling, a frieze in Wedgwood jasperware, a built-in sideboard with niches for jasper urns, and a neo-classical marble mantelpiece set with jasper medallions (Fig. 8); the bedrooms were given Wedgwood chimney-pieces with Jasperware plaques and clocks.[141] A new colour was created by

Figure 8 *The dining room at Buckminster Hall in 1886.*

136 Buckminster Estate Arch., black binder; TNA, WORK 14/1900.
137 Pevsner, *Leics.*, 117n.
138 *Grantham Jnl*, 14 May 1881.
139 Ricardo, ff. 281–4.
140 Ricardo, ff. 281–4, 324.
141 Ricardo, ff. 144, 149, 152, 163, 165, 167, 174, 186, 211, 212, 215, 216, 219, 220, 221, 224, 226, 236, 237, 262, 270, 271, 276, 277, 279–80, 281–4; TNA, WORK 14/1900.

Wedgwood exclusively for this commission, which became known as 'Dysart green'.[142] Further work by Ricardo included converting the old stables to managers' offices, and the brew-house and slaughter-house to a laundry block.[143] The total cost was £14,640, which was more than Lord Dysart had expected, and caused the relationship between architect and patron to break down irretrievably.[144]

Ricardo's estimated cost of £11,000 for replacement stables was not accepted. His revised design reduced the cost to £5,500, but was 'incapable of [further] simplification', and was rejected.[145] Two alternative elevations produced by J.B. Everard of Leicester also differ from the eventual building.[146]

The Hall was not occupied again after the death of the 9th earl in 1935, other than between 1940 and 1945, when it became an annex to Grantham hospital, with 100 beds for convalescent patients.[147] For the duration of the conflict, the dairy became a jam-making centre, and the exotic flowers in the conservatory were replaced with tomatoes, for local sale.[148] Sir Lyonel (4th bart) 'tried in vain' after 1945 'to find anyone willing to take Buckminster Hall', and in 1950 tenders were invited for its complete demolition and clearance.[149] The mansion was named in parliament as part of a regrettable 'tide of destruction' sweeping over English country houses, and was quickly scheduled under the Town and Country Planning Act as a building of special architectural or historic interest.[150] The Ministry of Works visited, but recommended only that the Wedgwood works might be of value, and should be carefully removed before demolition began.[151] The dining room fittings were sold to an American art dealer and shipped to Philadelphia; in 2014 these resided in a museum of art.[152] Fire broke out in the roof while demolition was in progress, but was soon brought under control.[153] The stone, '200 tons of well-seasoned timber' and '20 tons of firewood' were advertised for sale in 1951.[154]

The Surrounding Parkland

Contrary to Repton's recommendation, the Hall was built on the highest land, commanding a fine view to the west and north-west. As much of the land in sight was owned by others, Repton stressed that 'much of our improvement will depend on plantations'.[155] Woodland known as The Rookery and part of the Bottom Plantation had been planted by 1806 (Map 4). By 1829, the parkland between the house and Cringle

142 TNA, WORK 14/1900, 26 Sept. 1950; www.artsbma.org/pieces/mantelpiece/ (accessed 24 Oct. 2014).
143 Ricardo, ff. 149, 151, 154, 262.
144 Ricardo, ff. 317, 320, 322–3, 324, 336 (costs), 289–92, 294–7, 306–7, 314–16, 342, 345, 347, 367, 380.
145 Ricardo, ff. 173, 298, 336, 353.
146 ROLLR, DE 3736/box 39.
147 *Grantham Jnl*, 13 Sep. 1940.
148 Ibid., 19 Jul. 1940; inf. from Geoff Dunkley, son of Edward Dunkley (head gardener, 1909–52) [2015].
149 TNA, WORK 14/1900, letter, 21 Sept. 1950; *Grantham Jnl*, 24 Mar. 1950.
150 *Nottingham Eve. Post*, 16 Jun. 1950.
151 TNA, WORK 14/1900, note following visit 26 Sept. 1950.
152 www.artsbma.org/pieces/mantelpiece/ (accessed 24 Oct. 2014).
153 *Grantham Jnl*, 22 Jun. 1951.
154 Ibid., 7 Dec. 1951.
155 Buckminster Estate Arch., item 7.

Brook measured 227 a.[156] The park was stocked with 300 deer in 1833.[157] Deer continued to graze in 1878; 'cattle' are mentioned in 1881, and by 1910 it was let annually for seasonal grazing.[158]

Ricardo added 500 trees to the park, probably including many within the parkland and the shrubbery known as the Elysian Fields.[159] Gorse Plantation, to the east of the park, was added between 1885 and 1902.[160] The walled garden, of late 18th-century brick, is probably contemporaneous with the hall. A dividing wall was added by 1885, probably as part of Ricardo's alterations.[161] A greenhouse and conservatory were added in 1882.[162] In the early 20th century, the southern section of the walled garden contained vegetables, pear, apricot and cherry trees and redcurrant and blackcurrant bushes, and the glasshouses included a vinery and two peach cases. Grapes, peaches, nectarines and plums were then sent to Covent Garden daily in season.[163]

The House of 1965

After the demolition of the Hall, the site stood empty until 1965, when Wills, Trenwith and Wills were commissioned to design a new house. Known as Buckminster Park, the neo-Georgian house was built of red brick with stone quoins and dressings, with two bays each side of a central section of three bays, a hipped roof behind a blank panelled parapet, and Tuscan columns around the entrance porch and loggia. It has been described as Trenwith Wills's 'best completely new house' built after the Second World War.[164]

The Dysart Mausoleum

The Dysart mausoleum (Fig. 9) was designed by Halsey Ricardo in 1882, and is believed to be his only surviving work in the Gothic style.[165] Built in pink and cream banded and chequered sandstone,[166] it stands to the east of the church, beyond the original churchyard bounds, and is surrounded by iron railings. The exterior is mostly plain, with prominent stone buttresses at each corner, a steeply-pitched roof and a west door beneath a gable bearing the family coat of arms. A flight of steps from the door leads down to the burial chamber, which extends below the ground. The vaulted interior, of Ancaster stone and surprisingly richly panelled on the north and south, receives adequate light from the

---

156 Buckminster Estate Arch., Lordships map.
157 Surr. HC, K 58/15/149.
158 Principal Probate Registry, COW57116g; Ricardo, f. 157; *Grantham Jnl*, 19 Mar. 1910.
159 Ricardo, ff. 157, 173.
160 OS Map 25", Leics XIV.15 (1885 and 1902 edns).
161 S. Blaxland and S. Bailey, 'Leicestershire and Rutland Walled Kitchen Garden register, Buckminster Hall' (http://www.lrgt.org/download/ipmjss, accessed 6 Aug. 2016).
162 Ricardo, ff. 235, 244, 317.
163 Blaxland and Bailey, citing inf. from Geoff Dunkley, son of Edward Dunkley (head gardener, 1909–52).
164 J.M. Robinson, *The Latest Country Houses* (1984), 77–9, 204.
165 Ricardo, ff. 144, 148, 149, 166, 167, 171, 177, 185, 226; *Mausolea and Monuments Trust Newsletter*, 21 (2009), 2.
166 NHL, no. 1360830, Dysart mausoleum and railing: accessed 20 Apr. 2014.

Figure 9 *The Dysart mausoleum, Buckminster.*

east window, largely because Ricardo's recommendation of a stained-glass resurrection scene was ignored.[167] The building contains 45 loculi for east–west burial; the reputed cost was £3,000.[168]

A plaque on the west wall of the chamber, recording that the mausoleum was built 'pursuant to a direction contained in the will of William, Lord Huntingtower' who died in 1833 is not strictly correct. His will left instructions for a sum not exceeding £2,000 to be spent 'in building a family vault in the church at Buckminster', for his grave.[169] His funeral rites saw him laid to rest in a 'temporary vault' in the 'southern oratory' of Buckminster church, 'very near' the grave of his daughter Caroline, who had died suddenly in 1825.[170] His wife Catherine (d. 1852) and son Felix Tollemache (d. 1843) were also laid to rest within a vault inside the church.[171]

Burial acts of 1852 and 1853 ended the practice of intra-mural burials in urban churches, and the use of vaults beneath other churches fell out of favour. In his will, the 8th earl (d. 1878) requested burial in Buckminster, but left no specific instructions,

167 Ricardo, f. 171.
168 *Grantham Jnl*, 6 May 1882.
169 TNA, PROB 11/1815/62.
170 *Leic. Jnl*, 5 Apr. 1833; *Cambridge Chron. and Jnl*, 25 Mar. 1825.
171 *Grantham Jnl*, 5 Aug. 1882.

other than a desire for no pomp or ostentation at his funeral.[172] On his death, he was laid to rest in a temporary vault in the churchyard, with his trustees undertaking to 'build a family Mausoleum' on the border of the park, adjoining the churchyard.[173] On its completion in 1882, Lord Dysart's remains were transferred from the temporary vault to the mausoleum, together with those of Lord and Lady Huntingtower, Caroline and Felix Tollemache.[174] The other loculi remained empty in 2016.

The mausoleum also contains a wooden cross memorial to Lieutenant John Eadred Tollemache of the Queen's (Royal West Surrey) regiment, who was killed in action near Guillemont on 21 August 1916, aged 24, and is buried in Fricourt New Military Cemetery in France. He was the son of Sir Lyonel Tollemache (4th baronet), and the brother of Sir (Cecil) Lyonel and Sir Humphry Tollemache (5th and 6th baronets). Lieutenant Tollemache's death is also commemorated in the east window of St John the Baptist's church, Buckminster.[175]

172 *Grantham Jnl*, 5 Oct. 1878; Principal Probate Registry, COW 57116g.
173 *Grantham Jnl*, 5 Oct. 1878.
174 Ibid., 5 Aug. 1882.
175 http://www.cwgc.org/find-war-dead; https://petershamremembers.wordpress.com/2013/09/01/john-eadred-tollemache (accessed 4 Aug. 2017).

ECONOMIC HISTORY

THE FACTORS WHICH CREATE different kinds of employment can be intensely local. The villages of Buckminster and Sewstern had similar soils and a common administrative history, but adapted to their other circumstances in different ways. The proximity to roads and tracks, the changing importance of local routes over time and the ownership of land could encourage alternatives to the predominantly agricultural economy.

There were few differences between the villages in the nature of their farming. Each village had its own field system in the Middle Ages, producing a mixture of crops and supporting livestock, especially sheep. The open fields of each village were inclosed by common agreement in c.1600, when the parish became largely pastoral, with sheep remaining the predominant animal. The proportion of arable land, and also farm sizes, increased between the 1820s and 1870s, especially in Buckminster. There was then some reduction in arable, but land under the plough increased again from 1940. In 2017, almost all the farmland in the parish was arable, and mostly farmed by the estate.

There was little non-agricultural employment in Buckminster until the early 19th century. The creation of an estate village by Sir William Manners from the 1790s increased the range of occupations, including some clerical and professional positions from the late 19th century. In the 21st century, Buckminster remained at the centre of a large landed estate, which continued to offer direct employment, including clerical work. Additionally, the estate's commercial tenants provided alternative opportunities in a number of industrial and service industries. The road through the village from Melton Mowbray to the A1 also provided passing trade for Buckminster's general stores.

In contrast, by the late medieval period Sewstern's residents had taken advantage of the trading opportunities arising from their location near Sewstern Lane and Nottingham Road. By 1381, Sewstern had the appearance of a proto-town, with at least eight and possibly 12 craftsmen and traders.[1] Agriculture was still important to many, but the village's distinctive trading character continued until the early 19th century with, for example, building and glazing businesses and a tannery present in the 17th century.[2] Employments narrowed in Sewstern from the 1840s, when the railway ended the droving trade, although the rolling ironstone quarry face provided work for some between the 1890s and 1968. In the later 20th and early 21st century, the nearest non-agricultural employment was either in Buckminster, or on a small industrial estate just to the east of the parish boundary. In 2017, Sewstern still had a public house, but with no passing trade, the village was unable to sustain its own shop.

1   *Poll Taxes 1377–81*, (ed.) Fenwick, I, 600.
2   ROLLR, PR/I/40/263; PR/I/44/36; PR/I/58/14; PR/I/67/95.

The Agricultural Landscape before Inclosure

The complex boundary between the two townships, which included detached portions of land, provided each with similar levels of access to streams. The long, thin strip of Sewstern land extending to the northern parish boundary is typical of that encountered when woodland or heath is shared between parishes or townships.[3] The north-eastern part of the parish was on the edge of the Lincolnshire limestone heath, and was labelled as heath in a map of 1825.[4]

Vaudey abbey's grange stood almost on the boundary between Buckminster and Sewstern.[5] Most of the abbey's holding of 27 bovates (c.648 a.) in 1287 would have been in the open fields, but up to 19 grants of land to the abbey may be purchases or exchanges, which may have enabled the abbey to create an area of inclosed land adjacent to its grange.[6] Six closes in this area in 1840, containing 80 a. 2 r. 27 p., included the word 'grange', although this is not necessarily indicative of the extent of the abbey's inclosures.[7] Other than the paddocks behind the houses in Sewstern, there is no evidence of any other inclosures until 1532, when Thomas Bagott received the agreement of Kirby Bellars priory to inclose two pieces of land in the north of the parish.[8] These were probably in the vicinity of the later Buckminster Park.

Three open fields can be identified for each township by the end of the medieval period. A glebe terrier of 1601, almost contemporaneous with inclosure and mentioning an exchange of land, recorded 'one plott of ground in Wynterwell feld', adjacent to Nottingham Way, two pieces of ground in Milne Field and one piece in Lynge Field.[9] The glebe land was all in Buckminster, and the names Winter Well and Mill Field survived within the names of closes in 1840, enabling the approximate location, but not the extent, of two of the open fields to be identified.[10] The land in Lynge (Ling) Field was said to be next to Grantham Way in 1601.[11] This was presumably that part of the glebe land lying immediately south of Stainby Road in 1840, which is near heathland.[12] An area immediately north-east of Stainby Road was known as Stainby Lings in 1777, and part of Sewstern Lane near Stainby Road was known locally as The Lings in the 1920s.[13] The medieval Ling Field presumably extended north and west from here, into part of what became Buckminster Park, where ridge and furrow has been recorded.[14]

3   D. Hooke, *The Landscape of Anglo-Saxon England* (1998), 80.
4   ROLLR, Ma/L/29.
5   D.J. Rudkin, 'The excavation of an early medieval site at Buckminster, Leicestershire', *Trans LAHS*, 47 (1970–1), 1–13.
6   These grants are the only ones not described as being given in free alms: Rockingham Castle Arch., C1.7.21, ff. 51–55v.
7   ROLLR, Ti/53/1; Ti/279/1.
8   TNA, SC 6/HenVIII/1825.
9   Lincs. Arch., DIOC/TER/5, 168.
10 ROLLR, Ti/53/1.
11 Lincs. Arch., DIOC/TER/5, 168.
12 ROLLR, Ma/L/29.
13 ROLLR, Ma/L/31; inf. from Ron Skins, Buckminster resident in the 1920s.
14 R.F. Hartley, *Medieval Earthworks of North-East Leicestershire* (Leicester, 1987), 63.

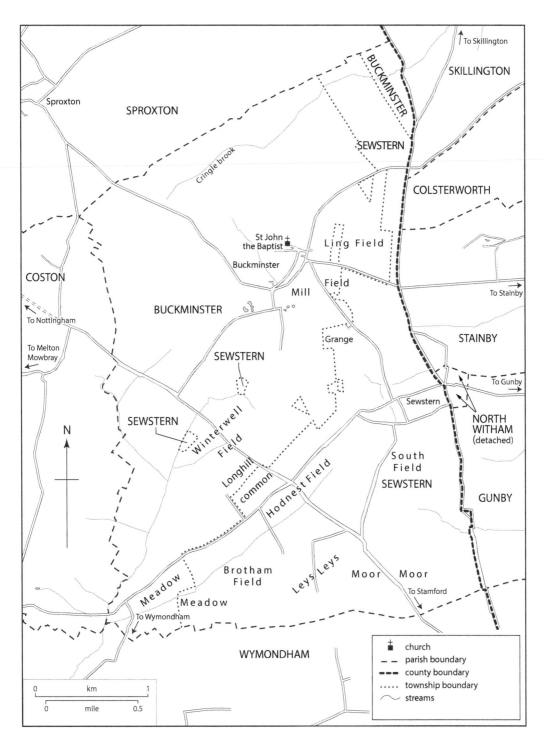

To Skillington
SKILLINGTON
BUCKMINSTER
Sproxton
SPROXTON
SEWSTERN
COLSTERWORTH
Cringle brook
St John
the Baptist
Ling Field
Buckminster
COSTON
Field
To Stainby
Mill
To Nottingham
BUCKMINSTER
To Melton
Mowbray
Grange
STAINBY
SEWSTERN
To Gunby
Sewstern
NORTH
WITHAM
(detached)
SEWSTERN
Winterwell
Field
South
Field
Longhill
SEWSTERN
common
Hodnest Field
GUNBY
N
Leys Leys
Moor   Moor
Brotham
Field
To Stamford
Meadow
Meadow
To Wymondham
WYMONDHAM

0   km   1
0   mile   0.5

✚ church
■
- - parish boundary
▬ ▬ county boundary
· · · township boundary
⌒ streams

Map 7 *Reconstruction of the agricultural landscape in c.1500.*

Sewstern's three fields were called South Field, Hodnest Field and Brotham Field. South Field is named in a charter of 1331, when it contained land butting towards headlands upon Littledale and Fulwellgate.[15] The latter two names survived immediately south of the village in 1840.[16] Hodnest Field was recorded in 1587, when it had recently been extended through the addition of land which had been part of Longhill common.[17] The name Hodnest did not endure, but five closes in the vicinity of the later Buckminster Lodge farmhouse (Map 3) containing 61 a. 0 r. 25 p. included the word Longhill in 1840.[18] This field may have extended as far north as Stainby Road. Another part of Longhill common was added to Buckminster's Winterwell Field in 1587, suggesting the villages may previously have intercommoned on this land.[19] Brotham Field was in the south of the parish. The name survived within a bequest by Thomas Bury in 1668 to his son Thomas of 'Square Close in Brothamdale', and an indenture of 1708, which included a close known as Brotham Dale, which was divided into three parts.[20] The name Square Close survived in 1840, adjacent to a close named Broken Dale.[21] Brotham Field included an area of common leys in 1587,[22] probably the small closes named common leys in 1840 (marked 'leys' on Map 7).[23]

Agriculture before c.1536

Buckminster

The larger and more profitable manor of Buckminster contained 52 a. of meadow and land for eight ploughs in 1086, suggesting c.800–960 a. of arable land.[24] The lord's demesne, with two ploughs, comprised about a quarter of this. There may also have been a significant amount of unrecorded pasture or waste, as Buckminster alone contained 1,796 a. in 1840.[25] The tenants had eight ploughs for their six plough-lands, and the additional ploughs may have been converting unproductive land into arable, resulting in the assessment of 9½ carucates. Their efforts may help to account for the recorded twenty-fold increase in the value of the manor in as many years, from 4s. in 1066 to £4 in 1086. The assessment remained at 9½ carucates in 1130.[26]

The annual value of the manor had increased substantially to £14 7s. 5d. in 1298, apparently as a result of increased rents. The lord's demesne had increased to 8½ virgates (408 a., as each virgate in Buckminster then contained 48 a.), while the villeins had 8

15   Rockingham Castle Arch., C1.7.21, f. 43v.
16   ROLLR, Ti/279/1.
17   TNA, C 66/1293, m. 13.
18   ROLLR, Ti/53/1; Ti/279/1.
19   TNA, C 66/1293, m. 13.
20   ROLLR, Will/1668/70; Buckminster Estate Arch., deeds 192.
21   ROLLR, Ti/279/1.
22   C 66/1293, m. 13.
23   ROLLR, Ti/279/1.
24   *Domesday*, 630.
25   ROLLR, Ti/53/1.
26   C.F. Slade, *The Leicestershire Survey, c.A.D. 1130* (Leicester, 1956), 22.

virgates (384 a.). Each of their acres was worth 4*d*., one-third more than a demesne acre, valuing their land at £6 8*s*. The eight free tenants paid annual rents totalling £2 7*s*. 1*d*., for an unrecorded quantity of land. With rent of 4*s*. 4*d*. from the cottars, total rent of £8 19*s*. 5*d*. comprised 62 per cent of the value of the manor, with the remaining 38 per cent within the value of the manor house and demesne land.[27] The manor was sold for 600 marks (£400) in 1316, suggesting the value was under-recorded in 1298, as this would equate to nearly 28 years' purchase.[28]

In addition to the gift of the manor of Buckminster, the foundation grant of the collegiate chapel at Kirby Bellars in 1319 included the crop from two carucates (384 a.) of land at Buckminster, the crop of hay, eight oxen, four cart-horses, four draught-horses, 20 cows and a bull, 200 sheep by the small hundred, six pigs, carts and ploughs, valued at a total of £47 12*s*.[29] This probably represented what was on the demesne, suggesting the land was then farmed in hand and ploughed by mixed teams of oxen and horses. By 1373, when labour was scarce following the Black Death, the demesne appears to have been let, with accounts showing income from rents and fines totalling £31 1*s*. 2¾*d*. from the manor of Buckminster and the grange.[30]

The poll tax of 1381 suggests Buckminster was wholly dependent upon mixed farming, with the 17 men listed comprising 14 husbandmen, two ploughmen and a shepherd.[31] There may have been other residents; this tax appears to have been evaded by many in this parish.[32] No detailed information is held regarding crops or livestock, but at Cold Overton (on high ground 14 miles south-west of Buckminster), the main crops in 1256 were wheat and oats. Wheat, barley, oats and peas were sown by the priory on their land at Kirby Bellars in 1399.[33] Like Buckminster, both these parishes have heavy clay soils, so the crops grown in Buckminster may have been similar.[34] There was almost certainly meadow alongside Cringle Brook and by the streams in the south-west of the parish. The mix of livestock may have been similar to that listed in 1319. Several charters record land in 'Buckminster and Sewstern', which may indicate an element of intercommoning.[35]

Neither village is mentioned in the surviving inclosure returns of 1517–18,[36] although the grange probably had some inclosed land by then. Post-dissolution accounts of 1539 for Kirby Bellars priory record no farming activity by the priory, which had income of £2 17*s*. 8*d*. from the farm of the demesne and £11 5*s*. 8*d*. from tenants at will. Arrears of 110*s*. suggest several vacant tenancies.[37]

---

27   TNA, C 133/84/2/3.
28   TNA, CP 25/1/124/50, no. 130, see http://www.medievalgenealogy.org.uk/fines/abstracts/ CP_25_1_124_50.shtml#130 (accessed 8 Mar. 2016).
29   A. Hamilton Thompson, 'The chapel of St Peter at Kirkby-upon-Wreake (Kirby Bellars)', *Trans LAHS*, 16 (1929–31), 167, 184.
30   TNA, SC 6/908/20.
31   *Poll Taxes 1377–81*, (ed.) Fenwick, I, 603.
32   Above, 22.
33   *VCH Leics*. II, 160–1.
34   http://mapapps.bgs.ac.uk/geologyofbritain/home.html (accessed 24 Mar. 2017)
35   Rockingham Castle Arch., C1.7.21, *passim*.
36   I.S. Leadham, *The Domesday of Inclosures*, 1517–18 (1897), I, 222–42.
37   TNA, SC 6/HenVIII/7311, m. 8–8d.

Sewstern

Sewstern was a smaller manor, with land for five ploughs in 1066 and assessed as five carucates, perhaps around 600 a. of arable land, with no mention of any demesne woodland, meadow or pasture. By 1086, the number of plough-teams had fallen to just 2½, one of which was on the demesne. As with Buckminster and many other Leicestershire manors, the valuation in 1066 seems very low.[38] This had increased by 1086, but by far less than Buckminster, from 3s. to 10s.[39]

Vaudey abbey built a grange in the parish by 1227.[40] In 1323, the abbey leased the manor of Sewstern and all its land in the parish to Kirby Bellars priory.[41] The priory had sub-let this land by 1373, mostly to tenants at will.[42] It would be reasonable to assume that the pattern of agriculture within the two townships was similar. A cartulary which belonged to Kirby Bellars priory, but which also contains details of grants to Vaudey abbey, suggests that the standard peasant holding in Sewstern comprised a toft, croft, one bovate of arable land (24 a.) and an unspecified amount of meadow and pasture.[43] The names 'peasland', 'peasfurlong' and 'flaxland' within this cartulary are probably indicative of crops grown alongside the main cereals.[44] Vaudey's land also included 'lez Waterforowes' (probably arable land with deepened furrows between the ridges to aid drainage), at least 9 a. of meadow and small amounts of 'holme' (an island or land which floods).[45] The abbey made substantial profits from wool in the 13th century,[46] and purchases or exchanges of land in the parish included the acquisition of pasture for 300 sheep by the long hundred (360) and pasture for 400 sheep and other animals. This suggests they had created a large pastoral farm in addition to their holdings of arable and meadow.[47]

In c.1529, Kirby Bellars priory exchanged 4 a. of pasture in Sewstern for 3 a. of pasture in Sewstern and 1½ a. of arable in Gunby.[48] The transaction suggests some pasture had been arranged in small compact blocks, or closes, held in severalty. The additional arable land was insignificant within the priory's landholding, suggesting this record may be the only evidence to survive from a much larger transaction aimed at improving rental income. Accounts from 1536 show no land was farmed in hand. The priory received £15 18s. 8d. income from tenants at will, 88s. from two fixed-term leases of the grange land, and the profits from a windmill at Sewstern.[49]

38   VCH Leics. I, 283–5.
39   Domesday, 643.
40   Cal. Chart. 1226–57, 3.
41   Cal. Pat. 1321–4, 356.
42   TNA, SC 6/908/20.
43   Rockingham Castle Arch., C1.7.21, ff. 51v–52.
44   Ibid., ff. 50v, 51v, 55v.
45   Ibid., ff. 51v, 52v, 55–55v.
46   VCH Lincs. II, 143.
47   Rockingham Castle Arch., C1.7.21, f. 51v, 52v.
48   TNA, E 134/17and18Eliz/Mich8.
49   TNA, SC 6/HenVIII/7311, m. 6–8d.

Agriculture between *c*.1536 and 1790

A sale of 620 a. in 'Buckminster and Sewstern' by Henry Digby to Henry Allen in 1549 included 300 a. of arable, 200 a. of pasture and 100 a. of meadow,[50] and these proportions may reflect those seen across the parish. As well as the cultivated land, there was also gorse and furze, a valuable commodity which tenants were prohibited from giving to anyone outside the manor under a by-law of 1550.[51] By-laws concerning trespass appear to have been widely ignored. The manor courts heard cases in 1550 and 1551 against some of the wealthiest residents, including vicar Thomas Watson, of leading unyoked oxen into the 'several fields'.[52] In these instances, 'several' probably referred to the large section of open fields fenced off to protect the growing corn, rather than private inclosures.

Very few probate inventories survive before 1550, and the 1535 inventory of Buckminster husbandman Robert Loryngton, whose only crops were wheat and rye, may be anomalous.[53] Mention in a by-law of 1550 of 'le Wheytfelde and Rye felde' could refer to just one of the open fields,[54] as both these crops would be sown in winter. In this period, barley was the staple crop on the clay soils of Lincolnshire,[55] and was clearly the main arable crop in Buckminster from 1550, when probate inventories become numerous. Peas were also widely grown, but there seems only to have been a small acreage of winter-sown cereals. Thomas Chrystyan was Sewstern's largest landholder in 1532.[56] At his death in 1551 he was growing 10 a. of barley, 10 a. of peas, 4 a. of rye, 1 a. of wheat and 1 a. of oats, and had five horses, two oxen, 59 sheep, 12 head of cattle and some pigs.[57] When he died in 1567, Thomas Shershawe of Sewstern was cultivating 17½ a. of barley, 9 a. of peas, but only 2½ a. of oats, 4 a. of rye and 1½ a. of wheat.[58] Buckminster's vicar Thomas Watson owned two oxen, six horses, 52 sheep, 14 cattle and five pigs when he died in 1551. He had no growing crops, but held 21 quarters and one strike of barley, six quarters of malt, seven quarters and 1½ strikes of peas and six strikes of oats.[59]

The former Vaudey abbey land probably included significant inclosed pasture, and some of this may have been bought or rented by Buckminster yeoman Simon Collyn, who was grazing 80 sheep, 14 cows, four oxen and other livestock in 1560, but had just 7 a. in total of wheat, rye, peas and oats.[60] The stint in 1551 was 50 sheep and four mares for each virgate (48 a.), and a by-law of 1550 forbade anyone to keep their flock with a by-herd (presumably a private shepherd). The following year it was recorded that no one

---

50   TNA, CP 25/2/60/459/2/3EdwVIHil, rot. 29–29d.
51   TNA, SC 2/183/54.
52   TNA, SC 2/183/54; SC 2/195/79, m. 4r.
53   ROLLR, W & I file, 1535/34A.
54   TNA, SC 2/183/54.
55   J. Thirsk, *English Peasant Farming* (1957), 102–3.
56   TNA, SC 6/HenVIII/1825, rot. 6.
57   ROLLR, PR/I/3/169/22.
58   ROLLR, W & I file, 1567/108.
59   ROLLR, W & I file, 1551/92.
60   ROLLR, PR/I/1/29.

could keep fewer than 200 sheep in a flock.[61] The need for such a by-law may suggest at least one resident was grazing his sheep away from the common flock, and it may have been intended as a deterrent against further inclosure. No record of a stint for cattle survives. Buckminster village may have had its own 'town' bull and boar in 1550, and perhaps refused to share them, as Robert Watson was told to find a bull and boar to service the livestock of Sewstern's inhabitants.[62]

Some meadow and pasture was converted to arable shortly before 1587, including Hammerhill in Brotham Field, Sewstern, which had probably been meadow, and Longhill common.[63] This may have been part of a wider rearrangement of the fields, perhaps compensating for arable land elsewhere which had been turned to pasture.

The parish was almost fully inclosed within 20 years of the sale of the manor by the crown in 1590.[64] A commission in 1607 heard that Sir Thomas Cave and his son and heir Alexander had exchanged 889 a. of (presumably dispersed) land in Buckminster and Sewstern for 895 a. within the parish, perhaps in large blocks, as part of a wider rearrangement involving the lands of 14 other people in Buckminster (including vicar William Floyde or Lloyde) and 18 in Sewstern. These may have comprised all or most of the owners of land. There appears to have been general consent to this, including by lesser landholders, as 19 named people converted less than 10 a. to pasture. The exchange enabled open field land to be laid out in closes. As part of this rearrangement, 327 a. in Buckminster and 159 a. in Sewstern were converted from arable to pasture.[65] A few of the closes were very large, with at least four containing 60 a. or more, including 'the pasture ground around the house' of 126 a.,[66] probably the forerunner of Buckminster Park. The returns record the decay of only three farmhouses in each village and expressly state that the inclosures made by 16 of the tenants in Sewstern caused no decay of houses of husbandry.[67] There had been similar inclosures between 1595 and 1607 in the neighbouring parishes of Coston, Wymondham and Edmondthorpe.[68]

The change in the nature of farming across the parish in this period is highlighted within the sale of 1,000 a., with the manor, by William and Elisabeth Smythe in 1612 to Sir Alexander Cave. As we have seen, around half the land in the parish was probably arable in 1549. This sale in 1612 comprised 700 a. of pasture, 100 a. of meadow, 100 a. furze and heath, and only 100 a. of arable land.[69]

Inclosure enabled farmers to make their own decisions about the type of farming they wished to pursue. Freeholder William Coye held 137 a. on his death in 1606, all of which was inclosed pasture.[70] Many smaller farmers had no more arable than was necessary to grow the fodder they needed. Husbandman John Burton of Buckminster (d. 1634) had

61   TNA, SC 2/183/54.
62   Ibid.
63   TNA, C 66/1293, m. 13.
64   *Cal. Pat.* 32 Eliz. I, 1589–90 (L&I Soc. vol. 301), 155.
65   TNA, E 178/4010; L.A. Parker, 'The depopulation returns for Leicestershire', *Trans LAHS* 23(2) (1947), 250–3; *Cal. Cecil Papers*, XXI, 1609–12, 362–74 at http://www.british-history.ac.uk/report. aspx?compid=112482 (accessed 1 Apr. 2014).
66   TNA, E 178/4010.
67   Parker, 'Depopulation', 250–3.
68   Ibid., 243–9.
69   TNA, CP 25/2/314/10JasIEaster, rot. 18.
70   Farnham I, 232–3, citing TNA, C 142/299/160.

farming assets worth £74 on his death, with sheep valued at £11, cattle at £22 3s. 4d., horses at £10, two oxen, barley worth £4 and oats worth £1 6s. 8d.[71] The largest recorded flock in Sewstern before 1660 was of 50 sheep, held by John Brewster (d. 1636),[72] and the most cattle were on John Reddish's farm: five dairy cows, two heifers, three steers, two bullocks and seven calves in 1649, with just 14 sheep.[73]

Some larger farms had developed by the 1660s. Yeoman Ralph Parleby of Buckminster died in 1663 leaving a mixed farm with crops and livestock valued at £496 13s. 4d., including corn (£6), oats and peas (£50), 400 sheep (£272) and 49 head of cattle (£132), as well as household goods worth a further £163.[74] In Sewstern, Joseph Ayscough, who died in 1680, owned 21 cattle, 131 sheep and lambs, two pigs and four horses, and he was a maltster as well as a farmer. His crops included (unquantified) wheat, oats, peas and barley worth £35, and he had 60 quarters of malt worth £48, and a pair of querns.[75] James Cam of Sewstern (d. 1685) had growing corn valued at £54, 174 sheep and lambs, 20 cattle and six horses on his death in 1685.[76]

Agriculture from 1790

The pastoral nature of the parish is emphasised by the crop returns of 1795, which list 21 farmers with arable land, only three of whom had more than 15 a. of crops, and these were mostly for fodder. The main crop was oats (62 per cent), with barley (23 per cent), wheat (13 per cent) and beans (2 per cent).[77] The return only enquired about food and fodder crops, but flax and hemp were probably also grown, as there were hempdressers in Sewstern in 1762, and Poor Law records show payment for flax and hemp for the parish workhouse in 1809.[78] Numbers of livestock were not recorded on a parish basis, but auction advertisements demonstrate that sheep continued to predominate, with the livestock sold from one large Buckminster farm in 1805 comprising 376 sheep, 52 cattle, a bull and three horses.[79]

Arable crops became a more profitable option for some following the laying of field drains by Irish and other labourers across Lord Huntingtower's estates between 1828 and 1833.[80] By 1840, 32 per cent (830 a.) of farmland in the parish was arable, 55 per cent pasture (1,430 a.) and 13 per cent (324 a.) meadow. The proportions were similar in Buckminster and Sewstern, but there were striking differences between individual farms. Most of the smaller farms with less than 50 a. had no arable land. On the three largest farms, all in Buckminster and owned by Lord Huntingtower, William Borman's farm (269 a.) was 62 per cent arable, Joseph Glassup's farm (289 a.) was 53 per cent arable, but

71   ROLLR, PR/I/36/169.
72   ROLLR, PR/I/38/46.
73   ROLLR, PR/I/15/71.
74   ROLLR, PR/I/60/79.
75   ROLLR, PR/I/82/117.
76   ROLLR, PR/I/87/87.
77   ROLLR, QS 28/95; QS 28/133.
78   *London Chron.*, 14 Dec. 1762; Nichols, *History*, II, 129; Buckminster Estate Office, Overseers' accounts.
79   *Stamford Merc.*, 18 Oct. 1805.
80   Buckminster Estate Arch., items 42–4.

just 11 per cent of the 452 a. at Home Farm was arable. Lord Huntingtower had a strong interest in agricultural developments and his instructions for Home Farm included sowing red clover and parsley within the meadow that was to be cut for the horses, growing white clover for sheep, ribgrass for fat lambs, and planting one rood in 1838 with mangelwurzel.[81]

The tithe commissioners described a four-course rotation across the parish in 1840, 'so far as it is reducible to a system', but with such differences between individual farms, the precise acreages of the crops they listed cannot be the reality. Their schedule shows exactly a quarter of the arable land in the parish sown with wheat, one-eighth sown with each of barley, oats, clover, seeds and turnips, and one-eighth left fallow. Annual production of 4,150 fleeces, 1,600 lambs and 490 calves was anticipated.[82]

The commissioners believed the commutation of tithes would encourage farmers to plough more land.[83] Better drainage would also have had an impact, and by 1877, 40 per cent of the farmland in Buckminster and 43 per cent in Sewstern was arable, the 19th-century peak.[84] Agricultural depression and reduced grain prices then led to a reduction in the amount of wheat grown, although the acreage of barley and oats remained fairly stable, reflecting their use for malting and fodder. By 1917, only 371 a. of farmland in Buckminster (22 per cent) and 190 a. in Sewstern (16 per cent) was arable.[85] The number of cattle remained steady at c.700–850 at the annual June surveys, but the number of sheep declined slightly faster than the national trend, from 3,182 in 1867 to 1,701 by 1917.[86] Annual or longer-term tenants were not easy to find, and grass was let by the estate and by other freeholders on a seasonal basis from April to December,[87] including the land within Buckminster Park.[88]

As well as improvements to the village from the 1880s, the 9th earl was keen to create model farms on his estate.[89] Home Farm (renamed Manor Farm by 1942) and Church Farm (renamed Manor House Farm by 2016) were rebuilt or substantially improved between 1885 and 1902, and an additional barn provided behind the Blue Dog inn, in Sewstern.[90] One notable farmer in this period was Algernon Hack of Buckminster, who farmed 674 a. in 1881 in Buckminster, Coston and Grantham,[91] and was 'one of the most successful sheep-breeders in the country'. He won numerous prizes for his Lincolnshire Longwool sheep, and exported to the Argentine Republic.[92] Lord Dysart and Alfred Manners also won many prizes for their horses at local agricultural shows in the late 1880s and 1890s.[93]

81   Buckminster Estate Arch., item 4, letter 17 Apr. 1838.
82   TNA, IR 18/4399; IR 18/4611.
83   TNA, IR 18/4399; IR 18/4611.
84   TNA, MAF 68/533.
85   TNA, MAF 68/2243.
86   TNA, MAF 68/134; 68/533; 68/1103; 68/1673; 68/2243; 68/2813.
87   For example, *Grantham Jnl*, 6 Apr. 1889; 20 Apr. 1901.
88   TNA, IR 58/50854/19; *Grantham Jnl*, 19 Mar. 1910; 9 Mar. 1912.
89   S. Wade Martins, *The English Model Farm: Building the Agricultural Ideal, 1700–1914* (Oxford, 2010), 183–8; P.S. Barnwell and C. Giles, *English Farmsteads, 1750–1914* (Swindon, 1997), 58, 61–2.
90   OS Map 25", Leics XIV.15 (1885 and 1902 edns) and date tablets on barns in Buckminster and Sewstern.
91   TNA, RG 11/3185/7/67.
92   *Grantham Jnl*, 8 Jan. 1898; 9 Mar. 1901.
93   For example, *Grantham Jnl*, 17 Sept. 1887; 7 Sept. 1895; 5 Sept. 1896.

Figure 10 *Gathering the barley harvest on Old Manor Farm, Sewstern in 1907. Barley remained an important crop on the village's farmland in 2017.*

At the behest of the War Agricultural Committee in 1917, the Dysart estate produced a scheme for ploughing up pasture in Leicestershire.[94] The committee was 'authorised to take possession' of 600 a. of this land,[95] but the impact on Buckminster and Sewstern was modest. Just 127½ a. were ordered to be broken up in the parish, and 72 a. were taken over by the committee from a tenant farmer in 1918.[96] Between the wars, many of the smaller farms were sold, to create fewer but larger farms, with 26 farms of less than 50 a. recorded in 1927, but only 12 in 1937.[97]

The steady decline in the proportion of arable land continued after 1918, but was brought to an abrupt end in 1940.[98] Leicestershire had one of the highest percentage increases in arable land during the Second World War.[99] Across Buckminster and Sewstern, the War Agricultural Executive Committee directed the ploughing up of 208 a. in 1940 and a further 395 a. in 1941. The committee took over another 343 a. themselves, reducing the size of 11 farms. Ironstone quarrying also took land from two farmers. Italian and German prisoners of war and the Women's Land Army supplemented the

94   ROLLR, DE 1841/2, 6, 16, 24, 27, 37.
95   TNA, CAB 24/45/21, f. 69; CAB 24/44/54, f. 161.
96   ROLLR, DE 1841/2, 49; DE 1841/3,. 4, 30, 89, DE 3663/188/9.
97   TNA, MAF 68/3356, 68/3836.
98   TNA, MAF 68/3356; MAF 68/3836.
99   B. Short, C. Watkins and J. Martin, '"The front line of freedom": state-led agricultural revolution in Britain, 1939–45', in B. Short, C. Watkins and J. Martin (eds), *The Front Line of Freedom: British Farming in the Second World War* (2006), 7.

local labour force.[100] There were still 17 prisoners of war working in the parish in 1947.[101] The grass at Buckminster Park continued to be let annually for grazing during the war.[102] Manor Farm in Buckminster remained the largest farm, with land spread across the parish in non-contiguous blocks totalling 581 a., including 243 a. of pasture; 217 cattle and 372 sheep were kept in June 1942.[103] Residents recall the major difference between the two villages in the 1950s being the size of the farms. Most of the land in Buckminster was divided between a small number of tenant farmers employing local labour, while Sewstern's farms tended to be smaller, and included several smallholdings.[104] Cattle remained important; four of the ten farms in Sewstern in 1959 were dairy farms, but pasture continued to be converted to arable.[105] By the late 1960s, a typical farm in Sewstern would use half the land for cereal crops, one-third would be grass and the remaining one-sixth root crops.[106] These proportions were remarkably similar to those seen in 1549 (half arable, one-third pasture and one-sixth meadow). Across the parish, 56 per cent of the land was arable in 1967, 29 per cent pasture and 15 per cent meadow, with livestock including 688 cattle and 3,625 sheep.[107]

Between the 1960s and the early 2000s, as tenants chose to leave the land, the Buckminster Estate elected to farm an increasing proportion of its own land. Its main rural landholdings beyond Buckminster lay in the Leicestershire parishes of Coston, Garthorpe, Saxby and Sproxton, and in the Lincolnshire parishes of Gunby, North Witham, South Witham, Skillington and Stainby, all within five miles of the estate's offices in Buckminster. In 2017, part of that land was farmed by tenants, but c.647 ha. (1,600 a.) within the parish of Buckminster and a further c.2,500 ha. (6,200 a.) in the other parishes was farmed in hand by the estate, all as arable, growing a rotation of winter wheat, winter and spring barley, oil seed rape and beans. The farms in hand entered the Higher Level Stewardship scheme for a period of ten years from 2010, with an environmental focus on an increase in bird species across the farms through the improvement of habitat. This included the establishment of wildlife corridors and tree avenues, and the creation of areas of specialised planting, including small plantations and plants which produce seeds favoured by birds. The estate's farms were run by a team of nine people, with additional staff taken on during harvest.[108]

100 Inf. from Elizabeth Goodacre [2015] recalling the memories of her late mother Dorothy Exton of Buckminster Lodge Farm.
101 TNA, MAF 68/4205.
102 *Grantham Jnl*, 28 Mar. 1941.
103 TNA, MAF 32/378/275; MAF 73/22/14; MAF 73/22/21.
104 Inf. from sisters Ann Wild, Gillian Dexter and Betty Neal, residents of Sewstern in the 1950s–60s [2017].
105 Inf. from Michael Goodacre, retired farmer of land in Sewstern [2016]; TNA, MAF 68/4205, 68/4575, 68/5037.
106 Inf. from Michael Goodacre, retired farmer of land in Sewstern [2016].
107 TNA, MAF 68/5037.
108 Inf. from Richard Tollemache [2017].

Woodland

No woodland was recorded in Domesday Book.[109] The first documentary record of any wood is in 1532, when the tithes of woodland called Gresecroft were leased by Kirby Bellars Priory to Thomas Bagot.[110] Woodland of 20 a. was included within a land sale of 1549, and by-laws of 1551 refer to 'colyars', who were to prepare a cartload of wood or 'le Colle' [presumably charcoal] each Michaelmas.[111] In 1626, the villagers claimed the nearest wood was 4 miles away,[112] probably referring to Twyford Wood, near Colsterworth.

Modern mixed woodland includes Bottom Plantation, on the northern edge of Buckminster Park, planted in the 1790s.[113] Gorse Plantation, to the east of the park, was added between 1885 and 1902, together with further trees along the western edge of the park and behind The Crescent.[114] Some of the specimen trees on Buckminster's village green may also have been planted at the turn of the 20th century. There were timber auctions every eight years in the late 19th century: 85 lots of ash poles in 1883, 129 lots of ash with smaller quantities of elm, oak, beech, alder and poplar in 1891 and 130 lots of ash in 1899.[115] In 1931, 959 spruce and larch trees were felled and sold from Bottom Plantation and Gorse Plantation.[116] The mixed plantings continued to be managed actively in 2017.[117]

Mills

Buckminster

The earliest documentary reference to a mill is in 1319, when the 'mills' were given with Buckminster manor to Kirby Bellars collegiate chapel by Roger Beler.[118] These may have been a windmill and a horsemill, but the former may have burned down or fallen victim to neglect in 1388, when only the 'site' of the mill in Buckminster was let.[119] As the two manors had been combined by this date, it may never have been rebuilt. The tithe map shows a 3 a. close in Buckminster called Mill Field on some of the highest ground in the

---

109 *Domesday*, 630, 643.
110 TNA, SC 6/HenVIII/1825.
111 TNA, CP 25/2/60/459/2/3EdwVIHil, rot. 29–29d., SC 2/183/54, rot. 1d.
112 Huntington Libr., HAM/box 53(6), f. 175v.
113 ROLLR, Misc. 2a.
114 OS Map 25", Leics XIV.15 (1885 and 1902 edns).
115 *Grantham Jnl*, 9 Jun. 1883; 7 Mar. 1891; 1 Apr. 1899.
116 Ibid., 30 May 1931.
117 Inf. from Richard Tollemache [2017].
118 A. Hamilton Thompson, 'The chapel of St Peter at Kirkby-upon-Wreake (Kirby Bellars)', *Trans LAHS*, 16 (1929–31), 166–91.
119 TNA, E 210/755.

parish, and presumably the early windmill stood here.[120] There was no manorial mill in Buckminster in 1585.[121] By 1678, there was a horse mill, owned by John Flower.[122]

Sewstern

Sewstern manor may have had its own mill by an early date, but the earliest record is of a windmill and horse mill in 1539.[123] The windmill may have belonged to the manor, but the horse mill was operated by a Mr Baxter, the tenant of a freeholder in Sewstern. It was claimed that manorial tenants ground their corn elsewhere 'in the abbot's time', especially when there was no wind, and some had querns in their houses, leading to an order being made in the manor court that the tenants were to use the manorial mills.[124] The manor had both a horse mill and windmill in Sewstern in 1585.[125] The windmill probably then stood immediately north-east of the crossroads between Main Street and Sewstern Lane, where a corn mill stood in the late 19th century. It burned down in 1901, and was never rebuilt.[126]

Extractive Industries

Limestone

Limestone for housebuilding almost certainly came from Lincolnshire quarries to the east and north of the parish.[127] Builders working on the gallery at Burleigh House (Cambs.) took delivery of 32 loads of plaster from Sewstern in 1556.[128] The limestone to make this may have come from Gunby and had presumably been ground at Sewstern mill. There is no evidence of any lime kilns within the parish.

Bricks and Tiles

Payments were made to brickyard men and boys in Buckminster in 1831 and 1832, who were probably making tiles (field drains), which were then being laid across the estate.[129] A brickyard to the south-west of the village had come into production by 1840,[130] and there were small brick kilns in 1845 in a field immediately behind Cow Row.[131] William

---

120 ROLLR, Ti/53/1.
121 TNA, E 134/27Eliz/East5, rot. 1.
122 ROLLR, PR/I/80/20.
123 TNA, SC 6/HENVIII/7311, m. 8.
124 TNA, E 134/27Eliz/East5, rot. 2. The date of the order is not recorded.
125 TNA, E 134/27Eliz/East5, rot. 1.
126 *Grantham Jnl*, 23 Mar. 1901.
127 British Geological Survey, Leicestershire Buildings: https://www.bgs.ac.uk/downloads/start. cfm?id=2392 (accessed 24 Aug. 2016).
128 TNA, SP 11/9, f. 8.
129 Buckminster Estate Arch., items 42–4.
130 ROLLR, Ti/53/1.
131 ROLLR, QS 73/64; QS 73/66.

Benson was recorded as a brick and tile-maker in the 1850s and 1860s,[132] but there is no mention of brickworks in later trade directories, suggesting the works were only to meet the needs of the estate. Boys were employed from a young age, William King being eight years old when he began work in the brickyard in 1872.[133] The brick-press and other equipment were sold in 1873.[134] The brickyards reopened in the 1880s when bricks were needed to build the Crescent and the stables, with advertisements placed for a brick-maker and a boy in 1884 and 1886.[135] At its peak it was a substantial operation, with 8,600 bricks sold in one week in August 1896, for lime-kilns in South Witham.[136] One of the earlier disused pits was said to be 20 ft deep.[137]

Ironstone

An iron ore seam in the east of the parish was between 7 and 12 ft thick, with an overburden of between 3 and 15 ft, and could be dug without blasting.[138] Opencast quarrying became commercially attractive following the opening of the Midland Railway line from Saxby to Bourne in 1893, which ran from west to east, 1.8 miles south of Sewstern village.[139] In 1894, the earl of Dysart granted a 60-year lease over an area of 19,500 a. in Lincolnshire, Leicestershire and Rutland, including Buckminster and Sewstern, to the Holwell Iron Company Ltd, who owned Asfordby ironworks near Melton Mowbray.[140] By the time quarrying reached the parish, other landowners had little choice but to give their consent, as the courts could order compulsory purchase or a compulsory lease.[141]

Railway tracks were laid as each quarry was opened, to transport the ore and coal for calcining (heating the ore to remove the water content), which was carried out at central points within the quarry area.[142] With increasing demand for iron in the First World War, the Great Northern Railway constructed the High Dyke mineral branch line in 1916,[143] linking the quarries to the East Coast Main Line four miles south of Grantham.[144] This allowed the ore to be taken to the blast furnaces at Scunthorpe, which became an increasingly important market.[145] The Holwell Iron Company was taken over by Stanton

---

132 *P.O. Dir. of Leics. and Rutl.* (1855), 22; W. White, *Hist., Gaz. and Dir. of Leics. and Rutl.* (Sheffield, 1863), 343.

133 *Grantham Jnl,* 16 Nov. 1951.

134 Ibid., 7 Jun. 1873.

135 Ibid., 29 Mar. 1884, 10 Apr. 1886.

136 Quarry diary, South Witham (private collection).

137 *Grantham Jnl,* 4 Jan. 1896.

138 H.B. Hewlett, *The Quarries: Ironstone, Limestone and Sand* (Oakham, 1979), 25.

139 E. Tonks, *The Ironstone Quarries of the Midlands, History, Operation and Railways,* VIII, S. Lincs. (Cheltenham, 1991, 2009 edn), 13.

140 Tonks, *Ironstone Quarries,* VIII, 13.

141 TNA, HLG 89/783, letter 12 Apr. 1951.

142 E. Tonks, *The Ironstone Quarries of the Midlands, History, Operation and Railways,* I, Introduction (Cheltenham, 1988), 47; Hewlett, *The Quarries,* 25; Tonks, *Ironstone Quarries,* VIII, 42.

143 Ibid., 15.

144 Ibid., 11, 15.

145 Ibid., 15.

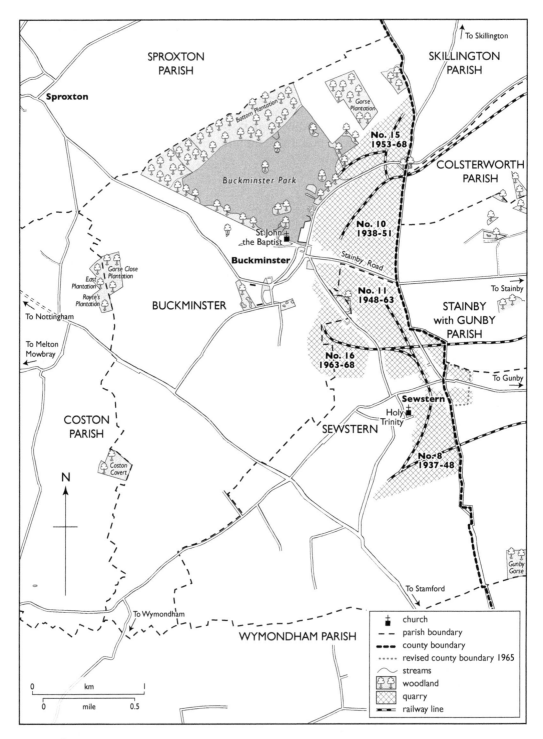

Map 8 *The ironstone quarries.*

Ironworks Company in 1918.[146] It became part of Stewarts and Lloyds Minerals Ltd in 1939.[147] The steel industry was nationalised in 1967, with all companies merged to form the British Steel Corporation, who were the operators of the site when quarrying ended in the parish in 1968.[148]

Because the overburden was relatively shallow, the land could be rapidly restored to agricultural use once the ore had been extracted. A dragline excavator worked one thin strip of land at a time, first removing the topsoil, which was placed to one side, then the overburden, and finally the ironstone, which was loaded into wagons and taken away by rail. The overburden was then replaced, followed by the topsoil. The entire width of the land occupied by the quarrying operation was only c.30 yd at a time, and each strip was only out of agricultural production for a matter of months. Meanwhile, farming could continue each side of the strip, on land which was yet to be quarried, and on the reinstated land at its new, lower level.[149] The breaking up of long-standing pasture encouraged conversion of the land to arable farming.

Quarrying began in Lincolnshire, reaching Buckminster parish in 1935, when a tunnel was driven under Stamford Road (Sewstern Lane), at the southern edge of the mineral bed and 750 yd south of Main Street, to extend the face into Sewstern (Map 8). The first of the five quarries to open in the parish (known as quarry no. 8) extended north from the edge of the mineral bed to the paddocks on the south side of Main Street, Sewstern, following the geology to the west, and was in operation between 1937 and 1948.[150] Although the usual practice was to quarry up to the edge of roads, Back Lane was also excavated due to the increased demand for iron during the Second World War, and reinstated on a straighter alignment.[151] No. 10 quarry was opened in 1938 in the north-east of the parish, bounded by Stainby Road, Hall Road and Sewstern Lane, and continued until 1951.[152] A mineral railway from the north took the ore away.[153]

In 1948, the mineral railway from the exhausted no. 8 quarry was taken under Main Street, Sewstern, and a new quarry (no. 11) opened up to the north of Sewstern village.[154] This extended from the property bounds on the north side of Main Street to Stainby Road, and was bounded east and west by Sewstern Lane and School Lane, leaving untouched only the houses and gardens of the three properties opposite the school.[155] This quarry closed in 1963.[156] Meanwhile a fourth quarry, no. 15, had opened in 1953 to the north of Hall Road, stretching from Sewstern Lane on the east to Buckminster Park, encroaching slightly into the park itself. This was initially served by an extension to the mineral line, but became the first quarry to use lorry haulage in 1964.[157] It closed

---

146 *Grantham Jnl*, 27 Jul. 1918.
147 *The Times*, 17 May 1940, 2.
148 Iron and Steel Act 1967.
149 TNA, HLG 89/783.
150 Tonks, *Ironstone Quarries*, VIII, 21, 22.
151 Ibid., 18.
152 Ibid., 22.
153 Ibid., 25.
154 Ibid., 26. The abutments of the bridge were still extant in 2017.
155 Tonks, *Ironstone Quarries*, VIII, 22.
156 Ibid., 59.
157 Ibid., 22, 27.

in 1968.[158] The lease had expired while quarries 11 and 15 were open, but quarrying continued, although demand had fallen due to the availability of superior imported ore through Immingham docks.[159] A new lease was agreed for 50 years from 1958.[160]

The final quarry in the parish, no. 16, opened in 1963,[161] and extended around and to the west of the school buildings, where the grange site was uncovered.[162] The only restriction was that the quarry was not to come within 50 yd of the school buildings without specific permission.[163] It was served by locomotive, by a branch from the former no. 11 quarry.[164] It was expected to extract 5,000 tons per week over ten years, but production rose to 11,000 tons per week, with the pit exhausted in 1968.[165] Quarrying within the parish ceased at that point, and the lease was terminated in 1973, following the introduction of a new steel-making process, which required ore with a higher iron and lower phosphorous content.[166] Around 100 people were employed in the quarries in the 1960s, including 30 engineers and maintenance personnel.[167]

When the final quarry closed, there were 3.3 miles of standard gauge railway line owned by British Rail and British Steel on land belonging to Buckminster Estates in Leicestershire and Lincolnshire, and a further 7 miles of track in the vicinity. The planning authorities were sympathetic to the concept of a preserved railway, railway centre and museum, coupled with engineering workshops to provide employment, particularly for ex-British Steel employees.[168] Buckminster Estates bought the track, and took over the British Steel workshops and locomotive shed on Gunby Road, just beyond the parish boundary. The first locomotive ran as a special excursion in 1973, sponsored by Grantham College of Further Education. A combination of factors caused the plans to be abandoned the following year, including a worsening economic climate, a withdrawal of support from Grantham Corporation, British Rail's wish to cut the junction between the mineral line and the main railway and the unwillingness of British Steel to lend ironstone mining equipment to the museum.[169]

Manufacturing

Sewstern's inhabitants appears to have taken advantage of their position on Sewstern Lane. The commercial nature of the village was evident in 1381, when a range of trades and crafts was recorded. The paddocks behind the properties on Main Street would have provided room for a workshop, a small close of flax or hemp, or overnight grazing for

---

158 Ibid., 59.

159 TNA, HLG 132/370, note 18 Jul. 1956.

160 Tonks, *Ironstone Quarries*, VIII, 13.

161 Ibid., 28; Buckminster School, log book, 1931–70, 192.

162 Tonks, *Ironstone Quarries*, VIII, 30.

163 Buckminster School, letter 16 Aug. 1962 in back of school log book, 1931–70.

164 Tonks, *Ironstone Quarries*, VIII, 30.

165 Ibid., 28.

166 Ibid., 37, 39.

167 Inf. from Fred Hand, former employee [2015].

168 TNA, HLG 132/58, meeting 23 Aug. 1973.

169 Tonks, *Ironstone Quarries*, VIII, 64–5; D. Ford, 'High Dyke and 4472: a preservation failure', *Heritage Railway*, 164 (2012) 64–8.

the horses of lodgers. Although wider than urban burgage plots, their similarity in form, coupled with their varying widths (indicating they were not simply former arable strips), suggests the lord's intention may have been to create a town and establish a market. The 43 occupations listed in 1381 include two wrights, a shoemaker, a smith and a cooper, and those without occupational designations include men with the surnames Bocher (butcher), Tailor (two) and Wright.[170] As Sewstern is 15 miles south of Long Bennington, the next settlement on Sewstern Lane, the village may have become well-known for its craftsmen and traders in the medieval period, and also able to attract business from travellers along Nottingham Road.

Little is known about occupations in the 15th and 16th centuries, but Sewstern's semi-urban character is again apparent from the 1630s. The most significant business was the tannery occupied by Thomas Bury, who died in 1668 with assets valued at £562 12s. 8d. His farm, with 15 head of cattle and 122 sheep, provided some of the raw materials for his trade, but he also held 340 hides and bark, together worth £250.[171] There was still a tan-yard in the village in 1708, and possibly until 1796, when the land was purchased by the trustees of John Manners.[172] Chandler and shop-keeper James Raven (d. 1633) had 30 stone of tallow at his death, with a shop stocking pitch, tar, starch, salt and soap, and a farm containing corn and hay valued at £9 13s., with 17 cattle, 20 sheep and horses, pigs and poultry.[173]

Services

Residents followed a number of housebuilding trades in Sewstern in the 17th century and beyond. Several were stonemasons. Thomas Blomfield was a glazier, and his probate inventory of 1662 included glass, lead, solder and a vice. He had no farming assets, but was wealthy enough to be lending £55, partly on bonds.[174] The only other service employments of any significance within the parish were the inns and work for the Buckminster estate.

Inns and Public Houses

One brewer, an ostler and a cooper were enumerated in Sewstern in 1381.[175] Two brewers were noted in Buckminster and three in Sewstern in the 1550s, all women.[176] Widow Mary Taylor of Sewstern, who died in 1681, presumably ran an inn, as her probate inventory included a 'signe and signe post', worth £1, and she had upper rooms called the green chamber and painted chamber, which each had two feather beds.[177] The inventory

---

170 *Poll Taxes 1377–81*, (ed.) Fenwick I, 600.
171 ROLLR, PR/I/67/95.
172 Buckminster Estate Arch., deeds 192.
173 ROLLR, PR/I/39/231.
174 ROLLR, PR/I/58/14.
175 *Poll Taxes 1377–81*, (ed.) Fenwick, I, 600.
176 TNA, SC 2/183/54, m. 1–1d; SC 2/195/79, m. 4; SC 2/183/95.
177 ROLLR, PR/I/83/34.

of innkeeper Henry Torr, who died in 1689, appears to relate to the same building.[178] An accommodation return of 1686 recorded one bed and stabling for one horse in Buckminster, suggesting the road through Buckminster was not yet of any importance, while there were eight beds and stabling for four horses in Sewstern.[179]

There were two public houses in Buckminster in 1784, with a third opening in 1797.[180] This may have been the first year that houses were occupied by Grantham freemen. The names of the houses were first recorded in 1827: the Blue Horse, Blue Cow and Buckminster Inn,[181] with the first two names reflecting the political affiliation of their landlord. By 1846 they were named the Blue Bull, Blue Cow and Durham Ox.[182] The Durham Ox had closed by 1855, and the Blue Cow by 1863, leaving only the Blue Bull, by the village green.[183] The Petty Sessions agreed that this could be replaced by a hotel on a new site in 1893,[184] and the Dysart Arms Hotel on Main Street, bearing the date 1892,[185] became the only licensed premises in the village.[186] It changed its name to the Tollemache Arms in 1936, following the death of Lord Dysart.[187] It had six bedrooms, with estimated annual trade in 1936 comprising 36 barrels of beer, 800 dozen pints of bottled goods and 30 gallons of wine and spirits.[188] Demand for accommodation was limited, and the only residents at the 1901 census were the proprietor, Arthur Wells, his wife and two children.[189] It remained the only licensed premises in the village in 2017.

The drove road provided trade for Sewstern in the 18th century, and there were five licensees in 1784, falling to three by 1789.[190] There were still three public houses in 1846: the Blue Dog, Red Lion and Waggon and Horses.[191] The Waggon and Horses closed in the 1870s, and the Red Lion closed in 1956.[192] The Blue Dog remained open in 2017.[193]

Estate Employment

Lord Huntingtower provided employment for large numbers of labourers in the 1820s and early 1830s, laying roads, field drains and building houses, in addition to domestic servants, gardeners, a gamekeeper and grooms at Buckminster Park.[194] The 8th earl and his family were resident at the 1841 census, with seven male and four female servants,

178 ROLLR, PR/I/92/110.
179 TNA, WO 30/48.
180 ROLLR, QS 36/2/1/6–7.
181 ROLLR, QS 36/2/1/10.
182 W. White, *Hist., Gaz. and Dir. of Leics. and Rutl.* (Sheffield, 1846), 227.
183 *P.O. Dir. of Leics. and Rutl.* (1855), 22; W. White, *Hist., Gaz. and Dir. of Leics. and Rutl.* (Sheffield, 1863), 343; Northants. RO, MF 594; *Grantham Jnl*, 2 Jun. 1883; *Stamford Merc.* 14 Jan. 1853; 17 Feb. 1854.
184 *Grantham Jnl*, 24 Jun. 1893.
185 Date tablet on building.
186 *Kelly's Dir. of Leics. and Rutl.* (1895), 46.
187 ROLLR, QS 36/3/5.
188 ROLLR, QS 36/3/5.
189 TNA, RG 13/3013/30/9.
190 ROLLR, QS 36/2/1/6.
191 W. White, *Hist., Gaz. and Dir. of Leics. and Rutl.* (Sheffield, 1846), 228.
192 W. White, *Hist., Gaz. and Dir. of Leics. and Rutl.* (Sheffield, 1877), 597–8; *Kelly's Dir. of Leics. and Rutl.* (1881), 499; *Lincolnshire Life*, Apr. 1970, 45.
193 https://www.facebook.com/TheBlueDogSewstern/ (accessed 12 May 2017).
194 Buckminster Estate Arch., items 4, 5, 42–4.

and he employed two agents, a farm bailiff, gamekeeper and gardener who lived in Buckminster.[195] There was then no resident lord from c.1843 until 1878, but the estate still had to be managed, and the house and grounds maintained. Up to six male and female servants were living at Buckminster Park in the 1851, 1861 and 1871 censuses, and there were also two agents, a farm bailiff, gamekeeper, gardener and night watchman in the village; an accountant first appeared in 1871.[196] The 9th earl was resident for part of each year from 1878, and expanded the range of employments, including a clerk by 1881, coachmen, stablemen, more house servants, further gardeners, an architect and architect's assistant in 1891, and a timekeeper, woodman, two surveyors and an electrical engineer in 1901.[197] By 1924 there were still c.14 gardeners, but the number fell to two following the 9th earl's death in 1935.[198]

The large estate, comprising residential and commercial properties as well as the farmland, continued to be managed from Buckminster in 2017. Sixteen staff were employed: a chief executive, managing director, three land agents, property manager, accountant, four other office staff and five staff with responsibilities for woodland, game and fishing. Property maintenance, including roofing, plumbing, heating and electrical work was contracted out, with about 15 contractors working on estate property at any time, and up to 50 in the summer months.[199]

Other Local Employment

The Buckminster Estate in the early 21st century was an active landlord, managing a property portfolio with the aim of supporting the local economy and providing rural employment. Some of the more imaginative schemes had been unsuccessful, such as the preserved railway, which would have created employment for former quarry workers, but the broadband project (2010) was ahead of its time.[200] This helped to attract new commercial tenants, including a media business, as well as making self-employment a more realistic option for some residents. Older estate properties have been converted and let, including the 19th-century estate workshops in Buckminster, which became office units employing c.50 people, the former forge, where a police office and architect's practice opened in 2016, and a former farmyard, which was used in 2016 by a welding and steel fabrication business. The diversity of the commercial tenants, which in 2017 also included a foundry, classic car paint shop, narrowboat fitter and sawmill, ensured employment was available locally for people with many different skills, as did the shops, public houses and village school, which also contributed to community life.[201] The economic and social life of the parish were closely intertwined, with the availability of rented housing, for example, helping to sustain the local primary school, and the daily school run by parents, in turn, supporting the village general stores.

195 TNA, HO 107/587/9.
196 TNA, HO 107/2091; RG 9/2304; RG 10/3298.
197 TNA, RG 11/3185; RG 12/2546, RG 13/3013; Cook's Dir. Of Leics. (1900) 106.
198 Inf. from Geoff Dunkley, whose father was appointed head gardener in 1924 [2015].
199 Inf. from Richard Tollemache [2017].
200 Above, 13–14.
201 Inf. from Richard Tollemache [2017].

SOCIAL HISTORY

Social Structure and Character

DESPITE BEING UNITED WITHIN A parish and having the same manorial lord for much of their history, the two villages had different employment patterns, and developed contrasting social characters. These differences became more marked following the decision by Sir William Manners in 1793 to move to Buckminster and create an estate village, and through the accretion of further land and properties in that village by his descendants. There are hints of unspoken tensions between the two separate communities from at least the 16th century: Buckminster people distanced themselves from the decision to sell the bell from Sewstern's chapel, some charitable donations were restricted to the poor of just one village, separate poor rates were raised, separate friendly societies were established and Sewstern chose to have its own parish council in 1894, rather than combine with Buckminster. The social structure and character of each village will therefore be considered separately, but in chronological sections, enabling developments in each village to be followed more easily, without hindering comparison. Where records do not identify a village, this is made clear, with the information included within Buckminster.

Social Structure to *c*.1763

Buckminster

In 1086, 20 of the 28 people enumerated in Buckminster were free sokemen, alongside just eight villeins, who owed services to their lord.[1] By 1298 only eight free tenants were recorded, with an unknown number of feudal tenants.[2] The villages were assessed together for tax in 1327 and were prosperous: only 17 of the 48 parishes in Framland hundred had a higher average personal assessment. Individual assessments were well spread, with a steady progression from 1*s*. 4¾*d*. to 5*s*. 11½*d*., the latter for Hugh Bond, whose name suggests that he was of peasant stock.[3] All those living in Buckminster village in 1381 earned their living from agriculture, but this was not a closed community.[4] Holders of land in 'Buckminster and Sewstern' between the 13th and 15th centuries lived

1   *Domesday*, 630, 643.
2   TNA, C 133/84/2/3.
3   W.G.D. Fletcher, 'The earliest Leicestershire lay subsidy roll, 1327', *Assoc. Archit. Soc. Rep. & Papers*, 19 (1887–8), 211–32.
4   *Poll Taxes 1377–81*, (ed.) Fenwick, I, 603.

in Long Clawson, Somerby and Wymondham (all Leics.), Billingborough, Colsterworth, Harlaxton (a 'merchant'), Pinchbeck, Stainby and Stroxton (all Lincs.).[5]

The dissolutions of Vaudey abbey and Kirby Bellars priory in 1536 resulted in short-term economic and social upheaval, evidenced by migration and a significant decline in declared taxable wealth within the parish. The villages were assessed separately for tax in 1524,[6] but together in 1543–4.[7] Nationally, the tax of 1543–4 yielded more than that of 1524,[8] but the number of taxpayers in Buckminster and Sewstern fell from 47 to 42, the taxable value of their assets fell sharply from £225 to £145, and the total tax assessment was halved.[9] The greatest change was among taxpayers assessed on assets valued at over £5, whose number fell from 14 to five; the number assessed at £3–5 increased from ten to 13, while the number paying tax on assets valued at less than £3 increased slightly from 23 to 24.

The 42 taxpayers in 1544 may represent two-thirds of families, as there were 63 households in the parish in 1563.[10] Very few surnames appear in both 1524 and 1544, and the wealthiest residents (or their families) appear to have moved away by 1544, with others taking their place. No one paid tax on land in 1524, when the religious houses had substantial landholdings, but widow Barkeley had land worth £20 annually in 1544, and Richard Tyer had land worth £2 annually; neither surname appears in the 1524 lists. Widow Barkeley may have been married to Sir Maurice Berkeley, who had died in 1522, and who had owned the manors of Coston and Wymondham.[11] She was living in Buckminster's manor house in 1532.[12] Richard Tyer was living in Sewstern at his death in 1556.[13]

The ownership of the manor by the Hartopp family from 1615 to 1763,[14] and the long incumbency of the Dixon family as vicars between 1641 and 1764,[15] provided some measure of social stability. By 1670 there were several prosperous families in Buckminster village living alongside others who were poor. Five of Buckminster's 35 houses had five or more hearths, including Sir John Hartopp's manor house with fifteen hearths; there were also five houses with three or four hearths, and 25 (71 per cent) with one or two hearths. The occupants of ten houses (29 per cent of the total) were too poor to pay hearth tax.[16] The more prosperous residents included the Parleby family: Mr Parleby's house had six hearths and widow Parleby's house had four. They were probably

5   Rockingham Castle Arch., C1.7.21. These charters give neither the date nor the witnesses.
6   TNA, E 179/133/108, rot. 3.
7   TNA, E 179/133/135, rot. 5.
8   M. Jurkowski, C.L. Smith and D. Crook, *Lay Taxes in England and Wales, 1188–1688* (Kew, 1998), 139, 144.
9   TNA, E 179/133/108, rot 3; E 179/133/135, rot 5–5d.
10   A. Dyer and D.M. Palliser (eds), *The Diocesan Population Returns for 1563 and 1603* (Oxford, 2005), 192, 215–16.
11   ROLLR, Wills Register 1515–26/154–7; Nichols, History, II, 143–4, 400–401, 413–4.
12   TNA, C 3/110/4; C 78/39 m. 13.
13   ROLLR, W & I file 1556/169–70.
14   Above, 29–30.
15   Below, 88–9.
16   TNA, E 179/240/79, rot. 8d.

the son and widow of yeoman Ralph Parleby, who had died in 1663 with goods and livestock valued at £659 13s. 4d.[17]

Piecemeal land sales by the crown and others over the 16th century increased the number of freeholders in the parish, not all of whom were resident. At the contested county parliamentary by-election of 1719, 22 votes were cast by Leicestershire residents with freehold land in Buckminster township. All voted in favour of Lord William Manners, who did not yet own land in the parish, but his father, the 2nd duke of Rutland, had substantial electoral influence across north-east Leicestershire.[18] Later records suggest there may have been a further c.20–25 Buckminster freeholders who lived outside the county.[19]

Sewstern

In contrast to Buckminster, Sewstern had just one sokeman and six villeins in 1086.[20] By 1260 there were four free tenants, among a population of unknown size.[21] Agriculture remained important, but by 1381 at least eight of Sewstern's 49 heads of household were engaged in a variety of other crafts and trades.[22] Perhaps as a result, Sewstern was the wealthier village in 1524, with a total tax assessment of £127 13s. 4d. against Buckminster's £97 6s. 8d. Sixteen residents were assessed on goods with a taxable value of £3 or more, against just seven such taxpayers in Buckminster.[23] Although there was an overall reduction in tax paid across the parish in 1544, some Sewstern residents had prospered, including Thomas Chrystyan, with goods valued for tax at £8 in 1524 and £12 in 1543–4, becoming the second highest taxpayer in the parish, and Simon Collyn with goods valued at £4 in 1523 and £10 in 1543–4.[24] Chrystyan paid the highest individual rent to Kirby Bellars priory (48s.) in 1532, and had goods valued at £53 8s. 8d. at his death in 1551.[25] Collyn was described as a yeoman 'of Buckminster' at his death in 1560, when he left chattels valued at £45 7s. 2d.[26]

The Glovers were another rising family. Alexander and William Glover leased former monastic land from the crown from 1575,[27] and Alexander had become a freeholder by 1602.[28] Two Henry Glovers (probably related) were among the wealthiest residents in the late 16th and early 17th centuries, leaving chattels valued at £140 12s. 5d. and £328 10s. 0d. at their deaths in 1590 and 1614.[29] One of the wealthiest Sewstern residents in the 17th century was a craftsman: Thomas Bury, a tanner, had assets valued at £562 12s. 8d. at his death in 1668.[30]

17   ROLLR, PR/I/60/79.
18   ROLLR, Poll Bk.
19   Univ. Leic., Special Collections, Poll book, 1775.
20   *Domesday*, 630, 643.
21   *Cal. Inq. p.m.* IV, 349.
22   *Poll Taxes 1377–81*, (ed.) Fenwick, I, 600.
23   TNA, E 179/133/108, rot 3.
24   TNA, E 179/133/135 rot. 5.
25   TNA, SC 6/HenVIII/1825, rot. 6; ROLLR, PR/I/3/169/22.
26   ROLLR, PR/I/1/29.
27   *Cal. Pat.* 1578–80, 142; TNA, C 66/1351, mm. 5–8 (1590).
28   *Cal. Pat.* 44 Eliz. I, 1601–2 (L&I Soc. vol. 349), 187.
29   ROLLR, PR/I/11/47; Lincs. Arch., INV/114/159.
30   ROLLR, PR/I/67/95.

Sewstern was similar in size to Buckminster in 1670, with 36 houses, 26 of which (72 per cent) had one or two hearths. There was no large mansion, but Sewstern had five houses with five or more hearths, at least one of which was probably an inn; the largest, occupied by John Thorpe, had seven hearths. Only 17 per cent of households in Sewstern were exempt from the hearth tax,[31] suggesting that trading opportunities alongside agricultural work may have lifted more out of poverty.

It was practical to have separate officers for each of the two townships but there are hints of an occasionally strained relationship: it was carefully recorded in 1550, perhaps at the request of those from Buckminster, that it was Sewstern's residents who decided to sell the bell from St Edmund's chapel;[32] William Chester's charitable endowment of 1703 to the poor of Buckminster specifically excluded Sewstern, and Thomas Bury's bequest of 1721 only benefited Sewstern's widows (see below). The separate charities may have resulted from the different economic character of the two villages, and an overall feeling of little common purpose, although a single rate was levied across both parishes before the 19th century.[33] Poverty in Buckminster was mostly linked to poor harvests, but some of Sewstern's residents were also susceptible to trade depressions, and might take on apprentices in better times, enabling outsiders to gain a lawful settlement and become a potential burden on the poor rates.

Sewstern's land was divided between many owners in the early 18th century. Fifteen Leicestershire freeholders voted in the county election of 1719 in respect of a landholding in Sewstern, all for Lord William Manners.[34] As at Buckminster, there may also have been a similar number of freeholders residing outside the county.

Social Structure from 1763

Buckminster

The lord of the manor, Sir John Hartopp, moved from Buckminster to Stoke Newington (Middx) by 1686,[35] and social leadership and manorial control almost certainly weakened for a period. The purchase of the manor by Lord William Manners in 1763 saw a return to strong lordship. One of his early actions was to purchase ten houses which had been built 'on the waste', but it is not clear whether these were in Buckminster or Sewstern.[36] Both villages had a substantial number of freeholders, who were mostly non-resident. Only 13 of the 42 freeholders with land in Buckminster township who voted in the parliamentary election of 1775 lived in the village, the remainder living elsewhere in Leicestershire, Lincolnshire and as far away as Sibson (Hunts.) and Bakewell (Derb.).[37]

Lord William and three of his brothers, John, Robert and Sherard, served as MPs, and he knew the political power a large estate could deliver.[38] He began to increase his

31   TNA, E 179/240/79 rot. 8d.
32   Below, 87.
33   Buckminster Estate Office, Town Bk; A. Fox (ed.), *Parish Government in a Leicestershire Village: The Buckminster Town Book, 1665–1767 and Constable's Book, 1755–1813* (Leicester, 2015), 37–8.
34   ROLLR, Poll Bk.
35   *Hist. Parl. Commons 1660–1690*, II, 503.
36   Lincs. Arch., BRA 1189/2/23, 58–61.
37   Univ. Leic., Special Collections, Poll book, 1775.
38   *Hist. Parl. Commons 1715–54*, II, 240–2.

landholdings in the parish, and his son John (d. 1792) and grandson William (d. 1833) continued this trend. It was the latter's decision to build a mansion in Buckminster, and his parliamentary ambitions for his sons, which began to change the social and built character of the village from the 1790s.

Comparing maps of 1795 and 1806 (Maps 1 and 4 above), it appears that Sir William Manners removed a number of houses along what became known as Hall Road soon after the completion of Buckminster Hall. He built Bull Row at about the same time, probably to rehouse the occupants of the demolished homes, and to accommodate new estate workers. Sir William had also inherited the manor of Grantham, which his grandfather (Lord William Manners) had purchased in 1768. Grantham was a parliamentary borough where both resident and non-resident freeman could vote.[39] The construction by Sir William of Cow Row in Buckminster, and Pig Row on the edge of Sewstern (just beyond the parish boundary), both by 1821, was probably with the intention of offering houses to Grantham voters.[40] Twenty-one freemen who plumped for Sir William's son Felix as MP for Grantham in the general election of 1820 lived in Buckminster. They included seven labourers, two stonemasons, a gardener, a painter and a brick-maker, who may have all worked on the estate.[41] Felix was not elected on that occasion, but in 1824, Lord Huntingtower (as Sir William Manners became in 1821) claimed that 'more than 60 [Grantham] freemen' lived in Buckminster.[42] In 1828, 'sixty new cottage-houses' in Buckminster were said to be available for Grantham freemen who would vote for his 'Blue' interest, presumably referring to the 62 dwellings within the Bull, Cow and Pig Row terraces, available through annual tenancies.[43] When the Reform Act of 1832 disenfranchised non-resident freemen living more than seven miles from Grantham, his 'entire colony' of 70 voters moved to Lord Huntingtower's land at Skillington, which was just within seven miles.[44]

Tensions developed between Lord Huntingtower and Buckminster's vicars between 1814 and 1832, culminating in a court case.[45] Other residents had no redress at law in 1828–9, when Lord Huntingtower found work 'in the vicinity of Buckminster' for a reputed 528 labourers.[46] Many were from Ireland, possibly from the estates of his wife's family in County Cork,[47] and lodged in the village. The combination of a high proportion of single men, overcrowded houses, less work for local people and religious and cultural differences created a tinderbox. Inflamed tempers led to the shooting of an Irishman in 1828, a riot against the Irish in 1829 said to involve 100 local people, and several lesser acts of violence and vandalism.[48] The death of Lord Huntingtower in 1833 brought these episodes to a close. Although living in Buckminster Hall in 1841, his son Lionel (the

39   *Hist. Parl. Commons* 1754–90, I, 326.
40   Census.
41   *Stott's Impartial Narrative of Proceedings at the Contested Election for the Borough of Grantham in March 1820* (Grantham, 1820), 43–62.
42   *Stamford Merc.*, 10 Dec. 1824.
43   Ibid., 24 Oct. 1828.
44   2 & 3 Will. IV, c. 45; *Morning Post*, 31 Oct. 1832.
45   Below, 89.
46   *Gentleman's Magazine and Historical Chron.*, Apr. 1833, 369–70.
47   *Complete Peerage*, IV, 566.
48   *Leic. Chron.* 18 Oct. 1828; 24 Oct. 1829; 7 Apr. 1832; *Morning Post*, 21 Nov. 1829; 23 Dec. 1831.

8th earl of Dysart from 1840) chose to live in his Westminster home after 1843.[49] Past tensions had been forgotten when he died in 1878, and the villagers expressed their wish that his grandson and heir would become resident.[50]

The 9th earl divided his time between Buckminster and Ham House in Petersham (Surr.), and played a large and positive role in Buckminster, changing its character from an 'estate village' to a 'model village'. Expenditure between 1878 and 1910 included demolishing Bull Row and replacing it with a circular development of semi-detached houses with large gardens and outbuildings (The Crescent, Map 6), providing reading and recreation rooms in the village,[51] a new village school, and a fine organ for the church.[52] He paid for short holidays for the church choir and music lessons for village children.[53] He also provided 'pensions' to longstanding elderly employees, distributed seasonal gifts to villagers, and bought clothing for children in the difficult 1930s.[54] Lord Dysart's employment of people from the professions, who rented his properties in the village, and his investment in the estate's farms, provided a class of people who could support his social leadership.[55] They included Algernon Hack, a tenant farmer of nearly 700 a. and prizewinning sheep-breeder, who held offices including alderman of the county council, rural district councillor, member of the parish council and chairman of the school board.[56] Col. the Hon. Gerald and Mrs Foljambe also rented property in Buckminster, and served as presidents or chairs of village organisations between 1917 and 1937, including the Buckminster Institute, the British Legion, Women's Institute, cricket club and garden fete committee.[57]

After the 9th earl's death in 1935, no member of the Tollemache family lived in Buckminster for 30 years. On the completion of the new Buckminster Park property in 1965, when the estate was owned by Sir (Cecil) Lyonel Tollemache, his nephew Lyonel moved there with his wife and young family. Sir Lyonel (as he became on inheriting the baronetcy from his father in 1990) and his wife played a full part in the life of the village, including serving as parish councillor, as churchwarden and school governor.

In 2017, Buckminster and Sewstern remained small rural villages standing among a cluster of villages of similar size. With Melton Mowbray just 20 minutes' drive in one direction, and Grantham a similar distance in the other, residents did not have to travel far for a wider range of shops and employment, or a night at the theatre or cinema. Opportunities for those without their own car were more limited, as public transport was infrequent, but the same could be said of many other villages in England.

Where the parish differed from many others was through having a resident majority landowner, whose family through many generations had kept Buckminster at the heart of their large landed estate. In 2017, the estate was managed by Richard Tollemache,

49   TNA, HO 107/587/9/10; RG 9/179/40/1; RG 10/365/47/27; *Grantham Jnl*, 5 Oct. 1878.
50   *Grantham Jnl*, 5 Oct. 1878.
51   Ibid., 10 Dec. 1887.
52   *Grantham Jnl*, 20 Aug. 1898; 22 Jun. 1901; *Musical World*, 5 Oct. 1889, 697.
53   *Grantham Jnl*, 12 Sept. 1885; *Lincs. Standard and Boston Guardian*, 3 Mar. 1951, obit.
54   *Grantham Jnl*, 22 Nov. 1913, 24 Dec. 1891, 23 Dec. 1899, 24 Dec. 1914, 24 Dec. 1931.
55   Above, 50.
56   *Leic. Chron.*, 3 Feb. 1889; *Grantham Jnl*, 8 Jan. 1898, 9 Mar. 1901, 4 Jun. 1898, 9 Mar. 1901.
57   *Grantham Jnl*, especially 3 Apr. 1937, 7 Aug. 1926, 15 Aug. 1936; *Nottingham Eve. Post*, 31 Dec. 1929.

with the aim of providing 'a thriving rural environment to live and work'.[58] This included private rented accommodation, a range of employments within the parish, working either for the estate or for one of its commercial tenants, a flourishing primary school, general stores, public house and modern village hall.

Sewstern

There were at least 32 freeholders with land in Sewstern in 1775, only 11 of whom lived in the parish, with others living as far away as Nottingham, Northamptonshire and Cambridge.[59] Lord William Manners and his descendants gradually purchased further land, but many houses and some farmland were owned by individual freeholders in 2017.

The Holwell Iron Company, which had workshops and a mineral railway just beyond the parish boundary in Gunby, recruited employees from the parish from the 1890s. They helped to foster a sense of community, establishing a workers' cricket club in the village in 1898, and chartering trains for excursions for employees and their families, for example to the Japan-British exhibition in London in 1910.[60]

Sewstern's villagers worked together to provide other facilities, most notably the Sewstern Institute in 1910, and their own village hall, completed in 1962. The distance between the villages made separate meetings a logical decision when a new school was required, but the separate workhouse arrangements in the early 19th century and Sewstern's request to have its own parish council in 1894 suggest the inhabitants felt they had separate interests, and perhaps little in common.[61]

Sewstern was the quieter village in 2017. Residents benefited from the facilities available in Buckminster, but had the options of either renting a house from the estate or home-ownership, with a range of freehold properties to suit many tastes and pockets. The village's roads, lanes and bridle paths were ideal for horse-riding, and some large properties had their own stables and paddocks, attracting purchasers seeking these facilities.[62] The two villages between them had a broad demographic and social mix, helping to sustain the services and employment available.

Community Activities

Most Leicestershire parishes had an annual 'feast' in the 18th and 19th centuries, generally combining a religious service to mark the feast-day of the church's patron saint with secular celebrations on the following day. It was probably the distance between the villages that led to Buckminster parish holding two annual feasts. Payments were made by the constables from at least 1755 to those 'gathering the town', acting as watchmen to deter crime or 'serving the poor'.[63] Following the adoption of the Gregorian calendar in England in 1752, Buckminster's feast was held on the village green on the Sunday after 5

---

58 http://www.buckminster.co.uk/ (accessed 1 Jun. 2016).
59 Univ. Leic., Special Collections, Poll book, 1775.
60 *Grantham Jnl*, 20 Aug. 1898, 20 Aug. 1910.
61 Below, 104.
62 http://www.rightmove.co.uk/house-prices/detailMatching.
    html?prop=23341848&sale=59859942&country=england (accessed 22 Feb. 2017).
63 Buckminster Estate Office, Town Bk; Fox (ed.), *Parish Government, passim.*

July ('old St John the Baptist's day').[64] At the vicar's request, the date was moved closer to the week of 24 June from 1886.[65] By the late 19th century, annual celebrations included sideshows, stalls, music, dancing and a cricket match, with 20 caravans staying for a week in 1899.[66] Sewstern's feast in the 1840s was on the Sunday after 10 October ('old Michaelmas day').[67] By the late 19th century it had expanded to five days,[68] and caravans and stalls occupied spaces on the wide verges and waste land of the village.[69] The feasts appear to have ended with the Second World War.

The Buckminster Horticultural Society was formed in the early 20th century. Their annual show lapsed during the First World War, but was revived in 1925, and was well supported with 1,038 entries in 1926. The event included entertainment, sports and fancy dress competitions for the children and an evening dance.[70] It continued to be held annually until the 1950s.[71] The show lapsed for a period, but was refounded in 1965 by new organisers as the Sewstern and District Horticultural Show. This remained an annual event in 2015.[72]

Even in 2017, the quiet roads in Sewstern were well suited to horse riders, including children, and some of the village paddocks had equine occupants. The annual Buckminster and Sewstern gymkhana and pony show celebrated its 10th anniversary in 1956, and continued as an annual Buckminster and Sewstern Horse Show in the 2010s.[73] There was also an annual one day Event with dressage and show-jumping for novice and experienced riders hosted at Buckminster Park in the 2010s.[74]

Lord Dysart provided a reading and recreation room in Buckminster for the benefit of working men in 1886, with tables for billiards, draughts and other games, newspapers, and a library of 250 books. Membership was 1*d.* weekly, and books could be borrowed for an extra 6*d.*[75] This was replaced by a new corrugated-iron building in 1895, named 'Buckminster Institute'. Membership was 5*s.* annually, or 1*d.* a week for 'lads and labourers' approved by the committee.[76] Desiring their own facilities, a public meeting was held in Sewstern in 1908 to discuss the provision of a reading room for the village. A committee and canvassers began a collection from both villages, and 'Sewstern Institute' had opened by 1910 on the site of the former village pound.[77]

Evening boys' and girls' clubs for children aged 8–16 were held in Buckminster in the 1930s and 1940s.[78] In 1953 televisions were hired so villagers could watch the

64   W. White, *Hist., Gaz. and Dir. of Leics. and Rutl.* (Sheffield, 1846), 227.
65   *Grantham Jnl*, 27 Jun. 1885.
66   Ibid., 24 Jun. 1899.
67   W. White, *Hist., Gaz. and Dir. of Leics. and Rutl.* (Sheffield, 1846), 228.
68   *Grantham Jnl*, 22 Oct. 1910.
69   Ibid., 17 Oct. 1896.
70   *Grantham Jnl*, 7 Aug. 1926.
71   *Grantham Jnl*, 14 Aug. 1953.
72   Inf. from Michael Goodacre, Sewstern resident [2015].
73   *Grantham Jnl*, 3 Aug. 1956; https://www.facebook.com/BuckminsterHorseShow/info/?tab=page_info (accessed 11 Apr. 2016).
74   http://www.buckminsterparkode.co.uk/ (accessed 11 Apr. 2016).
75   *Grantham Jnl*, 10 Dec. 1887.
76   Ibid., 12 Jan. 1895.
77   Ibid., 14 Nov. 1908, 19 Nov. 1910; ROLLR, DE 2072/111.
78   Inf. from Geoff Dunkley, resident in 1930s and 1940s [2015].

coronation.[79] From 1954, following a resolution that Buckminster Institute should no longer be 'conducted as a men's institute and billiards room', it became a village hall.[80] The unattractive corrugated-iron building was replaced by a new village hall in 2012, with an adjacent large car park.[81] It was used for a range of activities in 2016, including the occasional exhibition or talk, regular whist drives and weekly classes in bread-making. In Sewstern, village events were held in a barn on Timber Hill in the 1940s.[82] Fundraising for a village hall began in 1945.[83] Slow but steady progress was made, with £900 raised by the end of 1954,[84] and the hall was completed in 1962.[85] It continued to be used regularly in 2017, when overnight bookings were also available, with camping in the paddock behind the hall.[86]

Buckminster and Sewstern Women's Institute was formed in 1927 due to the efforts of Miss M. Fletcher, and held monthly meetings and an annual produce show.[87] Declining numbers resulted in the branch closing in 2001, although in 2015 the Institute's two prize cups continued to be presented at the Sewstern and District annual horticultural show.[88]

Village Sports

Regular games of cricket were played by a Buckminster team from at least 1857, and a junior club also played from 1860, which included players from both villages.[89] The ground was in the north of Buckminster, opposite the gardens of the Hall. The Holwell Iron Company established a club in Sewstern for their workers in 1898.[90] By 1940, there was a single club for both villages.[91] Matches were a source of controversy in 1948, when the vicar sought a public ballot on whether Sunday games should be played the parish: 76 residents were in favour of Sunday matches, but 153 were against.[92] Buckminster Cricket Club played matches in three separate evening and weekend leagues in 2014. Funds were also raised in the two villages immediately after the First World War, through whist drives and dances, in support of a cricket and games fund for the disabled soldiers at the training centre in Sewstern.[93]

79   *Grantham Jnl*, 12 Jun. 1953.
80   *Grantham Jnl*, 15 Jan. 1954.
81   Inf. from Alan McPherson, trustee [2015]; Charity Commission Register of Charities, charity no. 1135802: http://beta.charitycommission.gov.uk/charity-search/?q=buckminster (accessed 11 Mar. 2016).
82   Inf. from Michael Goodacre, Sewstern resident [2016].
83   *Grantham Jnl*, 5 Jan. 1945.
84   Ibid., 12 Nov. 1954.
85   Date on hall notice board; registered charity no. 521494: http://beta.charitycommission.gov.uk/charity-search/?q=sewstern (accessed 11 Mar. 2016).
86   http://www.valdirectory.org.uk/content/sewstern-village-hall (accessed 5 Jun. 2017).
87   *Leic. Advertiser*, 21 Jul. 1967.
88   Inf. from Elizabeth Goodacre, former member [2016].
89   For example, *Grantham Jnl*, 25 Jul. 1857, 21 Jul. 1860, 26 Sept. 1863, 14 Jul. 1860, 2 Oct. 1864.
90   *Grantham Jnl*, 20 Aug. 1898.
91   Ibid., 16 Feb. 1940.
92   Ibid., 19 Dec. 1948, 17 Dec. 1948, 23 Dec. 1948.
93   Ibid., 21 Feb. 1920.

The independence of the two villages was demonstrated in 1909, when separate meetings were held in both villages to consider establishing football clubs. Sewstern's team set up goal posts in the 'West End' field, while goal posts were originally erected on the cricket field in Buckminster.[94] They later moved to their own field with changing rooms, immediately east of The Crescent.[95] By the late 20th century there was a single team, Buckminster United, which played in the Grantham and District Saturday League in 2013.[96]

Country Pursuits

The Belvoir hounds began to meet occasionally in Buckminster in the late 19th century, beginning a long tradition.[97] Their territory stretched north from Main Street in Sewstern, to include parts of Nottinghamshire and Lincolnshire. The southern part of the parish was within the area of the Cottesmore hunt, which met regularly in Wymondham.[98] Shooting parties were entertained at the park in the early 20th century,[99] and shoots were organised by the estate during the season in 2016.[100] The former brick pit on the edge of Buckminster was fished by Grantham Angling Society in 2016, and trout fishing was also available on occasions in the lake in Buckminster Park.[101]

Social Welfare

Friendly Societies

Buckminster Friendly Society (the Old Friendly Society) claimed to have been founded in 1759.[102] It had 30 members in 1803, and admitted new members up to the age of 35.[103] Provision was made for members' wives from c.1832.[104] Anniversaries were well attended, with a procession to church behind a band, followed by lunch,[105] further parades and singing in the afternoon and evening.[106] Forty members left Buckminster Friendly Society between 1860 and 1865.[107] Some may have joined the Buckminster Amicable

94   Ibid., 25 Sept. 1909.
95   Info. from Michael Goodacre, Sewstern resident [2016].
96   http://www.granthamjournal.co.uk/sport/football/football-buckminster-exact-revenge-on-greyhounders-1-4863737 (accessed 11 Apr. 2016).
97   *Grantham Jnl*, 14 Jan. 1899.
98   ROLLR, DE 1/38 (A.H. Swiss, Hunting Map no. 7, 1893).
99   *Nottingham Eve. Post*, 14 Dec. 1910.
100 http://www.buckminster.co.uk/country-sports/ (accessed 11 Apr. 2016).
101 http://www.granthamaa.org.uk/buck.html; http://www.buckminster.co.uk/country-sports/fishing-2/ (both accessed 11 Apr. 2016).
102 *Grantham Jnl*, 24 Jul. 1858.
103 *Returns of Expense and Maintenance of the Poor* (Parl. Papers, House of Lords, 1805, vi), pp. 254–5; *Abstract of Returns of Friendly Societies* (Parl. Papers 1852–3 (31), c), pp. 84–5.
104 *Grantham Jnl*, 23 Jul. 1859; *Report of the Registrar for Friendly Societies* (Parl. Papers 1863 (449), xxix), p. 123.
105 *Grantham Jnl*, 23 Jul. 1859.
106 Ibid., 24 Jul. 1858.
107 *Abstract of Quinquennial Returns of Sickness and Mortality* (Parl. Papers 1880 (365), lxvii), pp. 338–9.

Society, which variously claimed to have been founded in 1839 or 1860.[108] It first appears in the registrar's report for 1864, when the two societies each had 47 members.[109] The Amicable was dissolved in 1892, and Buckminster Friendly Society also appears to have closed by 1900.[110]

Regular anniversary meetings of a friendly society were held in Sewstern between 1859 and 1872,[111] although it is not mentioned in any of the registrar's reports.[112] The Independent Order of United Brothers, Dysart Lodge, was established in Sewstern in 1884. It was affiliated to an order in Nottingham and London, and had 50 members in 1896.[113] It was last recorded in 1897.[114] The Red Lion Sick and Dividend Club had 89 members in 1929, with numbers growing to 147 by 1940.[115] It was still in existence in 1951.[116]

Other Forms of Social Welfare

There was a small clothing club in the 1870s, with 43 members in 1878.[117] A penny bank for children encouraged the savings habit, and had 33 members in 1873.[118] A close of 10¾ a. on the western side of School Lane, midway between the two villages, was laid out as 39 allotments by the Dysart estate in 1887, and known as Jubilee Allotments.[119] These were some of the largest in the area, and the rent was generally included within the cottage rents, or separately at £2 per acre, one of the lowest rates in the neighbourhood.[120] This land became a playing field for the school in 2000.[121]

The Buckminster and Sewstern Pig Club was formed in 1887, and Lord Dysart subscribed £2 annually for the first three years to help it to become established.[122] The objective of late Victorian and Edwardian pig clubs was to encourage working-class families to keep a pig, by providing insurance against the sudden death of a well-kept animal. Members generally paid a joining fee and a modest weekly subscription, and were often limited to keeping no more than two pigs. Pigs had to be healthy at the outset, and insured animals were permanently marked by an ear punch to prevent fraud. After

---

108 *Report of the Registrar for Friendly Societies* (Parl. Papers 1877 (429), lxxvii), p. 277; *Abstract of Quinquennial*, pp. 338–9.

109 *Report of the Registrar for Friendly Societies* (Parl. Papers, 1865 (410), xxx), p. 135.

110 *Grantham Jnl*, 21 Nov. 1891; *London Gaz.*, 23 Feb. 1892, 1014–15.

111 For example, *Grantham Jnl*, 28 May 1859; 24 May 1862; 25 May 1867; 18 May 1872.

112 *Abstract of Returns of Friendly Societies* (Parl. Papers 1852–3 (31), c), pp. 84–5; *Report of the Registrar for Friendly Societies* (Parl. Papers 1865 (410), xxx), p. 135; *Report of the Registrar for Friendly Societies* (Parl. Papers 1877 (429), lxxvii), p. 277; *Abstract of Quinquennial*, pp. 338–9.

113 *Grantham Jnl*, 4 Jan. 1896.

114 Ibid., 15 May 1897.

115 Ibid., 11 Jan. 1930, 10 Jan. 1941.

116 Ibid., 26 Jan. 1951.

117 Ibid., 18 Jan. 1879.

118 Ibid., 11 Apr. 1874.

119 Buckminster Estate Arch., hand drawn on 25" OS Map Leics. XXI.3; Buckminster School, school log book, 1897–1931, 331.

120 *Royal Commission on Labour* (Parl. Papers 1893–4 [C.6894–1], xxxv), p. 142.

121 http://publicaccess.melton.gov.uk/online-applications/applicationDetails. do?activeTab=summary&keyVal=0000820CM (accessed 11 Apr. 2016).

122 *Grantham Jnl*, 20 Feb. 1897.

a few years' successful existence, most clubs were able to pay the full value of a pig that died through no fault of the member, less the value of any meat taken by its owner.[123] Members of the Buckminster and Sewstern club paid an annual subscription of 2s. The club had a treasurer and secretary, and two [ear] markers and valuers were appointed for each village.[124]

Pig clubs were encouraged by the government during the Second World War as a useful addition to food supplies, but organised on a slightly different basis. By registering with the Small Pig-keepers' Council, owners who had tended a pig themselves for at least two months could surrender coupons in exchange for a licence to slaughter it, retaining half for personal use, with the reminder sold to a local butcher and made available to the public through the rationing system (which continued for bacon until 1954).[125] A pig club still thrived in Sewstern in 1949, when there were 80 members, including seven who had joined that year.[126]

Poor Relief

Poor Relief before 1834

Poor children were occasionally put out as apprentices within the parish, for example in 1709, 1736–9 and 1745.[127] It was decided 'by consent', when the annual accounts were presented to the vestry in 1765, that poor relief would only be paid in the parish to those who wore a badge identifying them as paupers.[128] Annual expenditure on the poor was £22 14s. in Buckminster and £32 13s. in Sewstern in 1776,[129] but by 1803 the cost had almost trebled to £61 13s. 9d. in Buckminster and £89 3s. 7½d. in Sewstern.[130] From 1806, poor widows were provided with coal, rather than cash, and other expenditure was designed to help people become self-sufficient, for example in 1807, when the overseers bought a cow for Robert Howett, who paid £5, presumably in instalments, towards the cost of £16 4s. 6d.[131] A vestry meeting of the whole parish in 1809 resolved to purchase a property to be used as a house of industry 'for lodging, maintaining and employing the poor' of both villages.[132] The building, in Sewstern, could house four families.[133] The overseers' accounts show payments for flax, hemp, spinning and weaving, and proceeds from the sale of cloth.[134] There are no records of spending on medical treatment

123 R. Malcolmson and S. Mastoris, *The English Pig: A History* (1998), 57–61; M.K. Ashby, *Joseph Ashby of Tysoe, 1859–1919* (1979 edn), 115–17.
124 *Grantham Jnl*, 7 Jan. 1899.
125 R.J. Hammond, *The History of the Second World War, Food*, III (1962), 727–36.
126 *Grantham Jnl*, 25 Feb. 1949.
127 Buckminster Estate Office, Town Bk; Fox (ed.), *Parish Government*, 21, 36–39, 44–45.
128 Buckminster Estate Office, Town Bk; Fox (ed.), *Parish Government*, 51.
129 *Report from committee appointed to inspect returns made by overseers* (Parl. Papers 1777), p. 38.
130 *Abstract of returns relative to the Expence and Maintenance of the Poor* (Parl. Papers 1805), pp. 254–5.
131 Buckminster Estate Office, Overseers' accounts 1806–39.
132 TNA, MH 12/6609/1838.
133 *Stamford Merc.*, 2 Oct. 1840.
134 Buckminster Estate Office, Overseers' accounts 1806–39.

or medicine for the poor before 1812, when 1s. was paid for 'a boy' to see a doctor.[135] The parish employed a surgeon from Colsterworth (Lincs.) to attend to the poor in the 1820s.[136]

Annual figures for maintaining the poor of each village are available from 1816, when costs had increased further and the relative position of the two villages had reversed, with Buckminster spending £204 and Sewstern spending £161 16s.[137] Although the Buckminster figure began to fall from 1817, in 1818 the people of Buckminster resolved to sell their share of the workhouse property to the churchwardens and overseers of Sewstern.[138] In 1820, Sir William Manners was letting three houses in Buckminster and six in Sewstern to the overseers of the respective townships, and three houses for each township in 1827. By 1834, a 'workhouse' was rented in Buckminster by the village's overseers.[139]

Buckminster's overseers reduced the cost of poor relief through agreements with family members, for example by agreeing to pay 2s. poor relief weekly to 82-year-old widow Ann Lambley (née Johnson) in 1822 against the agreement of Samuel Johnson of Hose to take her to his house at his own cost. He agreed that he and his heirs would keep her 'in sickness and in health' for the rest of her life, and would bury her, at no extra cost to Buckminster.[140]

Poor Relief from 1834

Buckminster and Sewstern became part of the large Melton Mowbray Poor Law Union in 1836, which contained 54 parishes and 56 guardians. The only parish representative on the board was John Firman, a farmer and landowner in Buckminster.[141] A union workhouse was built in Melton Mowbray in 1836.[142] The Sewstern workhouse was sold in in 1840.[143]

Charities for the Poor

There were three endowed charities for the poor. In 1703, William Chester of Knipton left income from land in Barkestone to be divided between the poor of six townships, with three-fifths apportioned equally or severally to the poor living in Knipton, Croxton Kerrial and the township of Buckminster, specifically excluding Sewstern. Part of the first year's rents was to be used to engrave his name on a pillar in each of the respective

135 Buckminster Estate Office, Constables' accounts; Fox (ed.), *Parish Government*, 199.
136 Buckminster Estate Office, Overseers' accounts, 13 Apr. 1820, 23 Mar. 1823.
137 *Report of Select Committee on Poor Rate Returns* (Parl. Papers 1822 (556), v), pp. 83–4; (Parl. Papers 1825 (334), iv), pp. 315–16; (Parl. Papers 1830–1 (83), xi), p. 98; (Parl. Papers 1835 (444), xlvii), p. 96; *Second Annual Report of Poor Law Commissioners* (Parl. Papers, 1836 (595), xxix), pp. 178–9.
138 TNA, MH 12/6609/1838; Buckminster Estate Office, Overseers' accounts, 1821.
139 Buckminster Estate Arch., Rental books, 1820, 1827, 1834.
140 Buckminster Estate Office, Overseers' accounts, 1806–39, at back of book; ROLLR, parish registers for Hose.
141 TNA, MH 12/6609/1836; W. White, *Hist., Gaz. and Dir. Leics.* (Sheffield, 1846), 227.
142 TNA, MH 12/6609/1837.
143 *Stamford Merc.*, 2 Oct. 1840; TNA, MH 12/6609/1838.

churches (Fig. 11).[144] The endowment comprised a farm house and 68 a. of arable and pasture, let for £126 annually in 1839.[145] From the Buckminster portion that year, the parish officers spent 14s. on Bibles for poor children, with the remainder distributed to poor people selected by the parish officers, in amounts ranging from 5s. to £2, with preference given to widows.[146] The charity continued in 2016, under a scheme of 1899, with a separate registered charity for the Buckminster income.[147]

In 1721, Thomas Bury bequeathed annual rent of £6 from lands in Sewstern, with £5 to be distributed annually to five poor widows of Sewstern, 15s. to the vicar for an annual sermon on St Thomas's day (21 December) and 5s. annually to the parish clerk.[148] Details of this bequest were added to the pillar in Buckminster church. By the end of the 20th century, with the value of the distribution steadily eroded through inflation, a decision was taken that the charity should be dissolved. It was removed from the register of charities in 2000.[149]

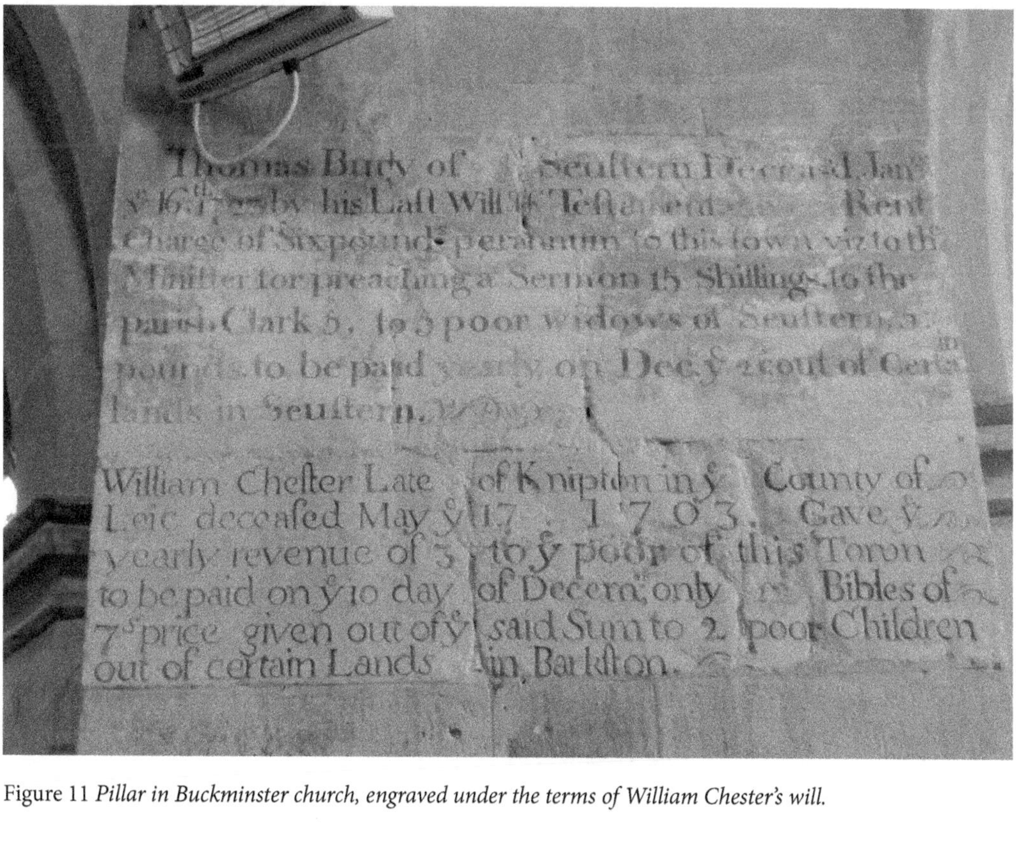

Figure 11 *Pillar in Buckminster church, engraved under the terms of William Chester's will.*

144 ROLLR, Wills 1703/39.
145 *Report of the Charity Commissioners* (Parl. Papers 1839 [163], xv), pp. 428–9.
146 Ibid., 435.
147 Charity Commission Register, registered charity nos 233327, 501347: http://forms.charitycommission. gov.uk/find-charities/ (accessed 18 Mar.2016).
148 ROLLR, W & IW & I 1723, fiche 2; *Report of the Charity Commissioners* (Parl. Papers 1839 [163], xv), p. 435.
149 Charity Commission, registered charity nos 248865, 248866.

Mary Elston of Buckminster left £5 in her will of 1724, the interest on which was to be distributed to the poor of the parish in bread on the feast of the Purification (2 February).[150] The Charity Commissioners noted in 1839 that the income had been retained for the previous 35 years, and the vicar responded by arranging for £20 to be distributed.[151] The money was transferred to the official trustee of charitable funds in 1876.[152] By 1910, 'by no stretch of connivance could it be made to go all round', but 28 four-pound loaves were distributed that year.[153] The charity was dissolved in 1998.[154]

Education

Sunday Schools

By 1818 the parish had two Sunday schools, one containing 45–50 children, and the other with 20 children.[155] Although neither village nor denomination was recorded that year, in 1833, a Wesleyan Sunday school in Sewstern taught 33 boys and 27 girls, and a Sunday school in Buckminster, probably attached to the parish church, taught 30 boys and 20 girls.[156] Both attendances suggest a preference by parents to educate their sons. On census Sunday in 1851, 54 children attended the Anglican Sunday school attached to Holy Trinity, Sewstern,[157] and 30 were present at the Anglican Sunday school at Buckminster, where the vicar commented that 50–60 children normally attended.[158] No Wesleyan Sunday school is recorded that day in either village.[159] The total substantially exceeds the 40 children recorded at the day school in 1848, whose parents paid a weekly fee.[160] Buckminster also had a Wesleyan Sunday school by 1857, attended by 80 children in 1859.[161]

Day Schools before 1800

It has been suggested that there was a grammar school in Buckminster in the early 17th century, as some local boys were admitted to Cambridge,[162] but they may have been taught elsewhere, perhaps at Wymondham, Melton Mowbray or Grantham, after receiving a basic education in the village. Probate inventories and the town book indicate a high degree of literacy in the 17th and early 18th centuries.[163] Four schoolmasters are

---

150 ROLLR, Wills 1725, fiche 6.
151 *Rep. Charity Commissioners* (Parl. Papers 1839 [163], xv), p. 435.
152 Buckminster Estate Office, Chester's charity accts, 1858–93, 69.
153 *Grantham Jnl*, 8 Jan. 1910.
154 Charity Commission, registered charity no. 248867.
155 *Report of Select Committee on Educ. of the Poor* (Parl. Papers 1819 (224), ix), p. 450.
156 *Education Enquiry* (Parl. Papers 1835 (62), xlii), p. 482.
157 TNA, HO 129/418/101.
158 TNA, HO 129/418/99A.
159 TNA, HO 129/427/22.
160 National Society, *Church Schools Enquiry*, 1847 (1849), Leics, 2–3.
161 *Grantham Jnl*, 8 Aug. 1857; 30 Jul. 1859.
162 W.A.L. Vincent, *The State and School Education in England and Wales, 1640–60* (1950), 125.
163 Buckminster Estate Office, Town Bk, 712; Fox (ed.), *Parish Government*, xv, 23–4.

recorded in Buckminster in the 17th century: Richard Paise in 1616,[164] curate James Stackhouse in 1639, William Clagett in 1665, and Samuel Taylor in 1667, the latter two being graduates.[165] No day school was noted between 1706 and 1718, but there were two dame schools for young children in 1721.[166] William Penford was licensed as a schoolmaster in 1762.[167] His school probably met in the north chapel of Buckminster church, which some people called a schoolhouse in 1795, although it was not then used for that purpose.[168]

Day Schools, 1800–70

There were two day schools for older children in 1818, one with 40–50 pupils and one for 20 children, and two small schools attended by a total of 19 young children from the two villages.[169] Only one weekday school was recorded in 1833, where 40 boys and 20 girls were instructed at the expense of their parents, but many could not afford the fee.[170]

In 1840, Revd Lawson conveyed one rood of glebe land almost mid-way between the villages to trustees for a National (Church of England) school for 80 children, who would be taught on weekdays and Sundays. A collection to cover the estimated building costs of £162 13s. 3d. raised £61, and materials were also donated. Grants of £40 from the government and £20 from the National Society were obtained.[171] Running costs were covered by annual subscriptions (donations) totalling £20, and weekly fees from the children's parents, set at 1½d. for labourers' children and 2d. or 3d. for the children of farmers.[172] The school opened in 1841,[173] and offered its first master a house in 1842.[174] Revised government standards reduced the capacity to 60 pupils in 1862, and to 48 pupils in 1867.

Day Schools from 1870

The school was too small to meet the requirements of the 1870 Education Act, and HM Inspectors recommended a single school for both villages, with 56 places for Buckminster children, and 41 for Sewstern.[175] A meeting of parishioners, called by the vicar, voted in favour of establishing a non-denominational school board to provide a new or extended building.[176] To their 'great astonishment' vicar Francis Rabbetts added a classroom to the existing Church of England school instead, although that did not

164 http://db.theclergydatabase.org.uk/?CDBSubscrID=53556 (accessed 3 Aug. 2016).
165 ROLLR, 1D 41/34/1, ff. 31, 37v, 38.
166 Broad (ed.), *Bishop Wake's Summary of Visitation Returns from the Diocese of Lincoln 1705–15* (Oxford, 2012), II, 755; Lincs. Arch., DIOC/GIBSON/4, 121, DIOC/GIBSON/12, 118.
167 ROLLR, 1D 41/34/5/248.
168 Nichols, *History*, II, 126.
169 *Rep. Educ. of the Poor*, p. 450.
170 *Education Enquiry*, p. 482.
171 CERC, NS/7/1/2206, cert. of completion.
172 Ibid., grant application.
173 Ibid., cert. of completion.
174 *Stamford Merc.*, 22 Oct. 1841.
175 TNA, ED 2/272, inspection reports, 1871.
176 *Grantham Jnl*, 3 Jul. 1875.

provide the places required.[177] In 1874, the government gave the trustees six months to provide a school for 100 pupils, or a non-denominational board would be established to build new premises.[178] The trustees failed to address the need, and separate meetings in the two villages both voted to establish a board.[179] This had three elected members from Buckminster, John Adcock (chairman, farmer), Algernon Hack (farmer), and the vicar, and two from Sewstern, Henry Manners (landowner and agricultural agent) and William Standland (farmer and Methodist preacher).[180] The trustees, all Anglican clergy, agreed to lease the school premises to the board, but with a covenant giving the trustees unrestricted use of the premises at various times, including 11.30am–2pm on weekdays, ensuring denominational teaching would continue.[181] The board objected to the terms and approached Lord Dysart, who offered an alternative site.[182] However, they finally decided to accept a lease from the trustees, to extend the premises to accommodate 110 pupils, and to build a new house for the master.[183] A government loan of £699 14s. 0d. was agreed.[184]

The lease expired in 1897. The school had needed to close three times in 1896 due to outbreaks of fever, believed to be due to poor ventilation, and a government surveyor condemned the whole building.[185] The parishioners were concerned that the rates would be too heavy if money had to be borrowed to build a new school, so the board approached Lord Dysart again.[186] He agreed to provide a one-acre site almost exactly opposite the master's house, and cover the capital cost of the building, provided that the school was non-denominational, was managed by a committee nominated by him, and that ongoing costs would be supported by villagers through a voluntary rate on owners and tenants.[187]

His offer was accepted. The new school for 120 children, costing £1,600, opened in 1899 (Fig. 12).[188] A new voluntary rate, set at 4d. in the pound, was collected annually by the schoolmaster.[189] Officially it was still a board school, and a new board was elected by the ratepayers, comprising Algernon Hack (farmer), Thompson Skins (blacksmith) and John Hawley (mason) from Buckminster, and James Baines (farmer and butcher) and Thomas Sharp (wheelwright and post office clerk) from Sewstern.[190] This board had little power, as a committee was also nominated in accordance with the earl's conditions, which met for the first time in 1899. Its six members were Lord Dysart (chairman), Wilfrid Praeger (Lord Dysart's secretary, who became secretary and treasurer to the school committee), Revd Astley Cooper (vicar), Herbert Bartram

177   Ibid., 3 July 1875, 17 Jan. 1874.
178   TNA, ED 2/272; *Leic. Jnl*, 29 May 1874.
179   TNA, ED 2/272, letter 29 June 1874; *Grantham Jnl*, 1 Aug. 1874.
180   *Grantham Jnl*, 31 Oct. 1874; Census enumerators' books.
181   CERC, NS/7/1/2206, indenture 30 Oct. 1876.
182   *Grantham Jnl*, 3 Jul. 1875.
183   Ibid., 27 Jan. 1877; *Kelly's Dir. Leics. and Rutl.* (1891), 547.
184   TNA, ED 2/272, note in 1901.
185   CERC, NS/7/1/2206, letter 4 Sept. 1897; *Grantham Jnl*, 7 Oct. 1899.
186   Ibid., 22 Jun. 1901.
187   Ibid., 20 Aug. 1898, 22 Jun. 1901.
188   Ibid., 7 Oct. 1899; *Kelly's Dir. Leics. and Rutl.* (1908), 51.
189   *Grantham Jnl*, 16 Dec. 1899.
190   Ibid., 24 Sept. 1898; census enumerator's reports.

(farmer), and one elected member of the school board from each village: Algernon Hack and Thomas Sharp.[191]

Although the village school catered for all ages, two boys from Buckminster School gained three-year scholarships in 1901 to a new grammar school which had been built in Wymondham in 1882, and which offered a wider curriculum.[192] Two more boys from the village school won scholarships there for two years in 1904.[193] Wymondham Grammar School closed in 1906.[194] Melton Mowbray Grammar School offered its first free places to Buckminster and Sewstern children in 1921.[195]

Management of Buckminster School was transferred to the Education Department of Leicestershire County Council in 1910, under the terms of the 1902 Education Act.[196] As other village primary schools closed over the 20th century, Buckminster School benefited from a widening catchment area. After the Second World War, all its pupils transferred to a secondary school in either Melton Mowbray or Grantham at the age of 11. With the addition of new classrooms, the 1898 school continued to serve the

Figure 12 *Buckminster 'Undenominational' School of 1898.*

191 Ibid., 7 Oct. 1899.
192 *Leic. Chron.* 30 Sept. 1882.
193 Buckminster School, log book 1897–1931, 83, 135.
194 *Grantham Jnl*, 25 Feb. 1905.
195 Buckminster School, log book 1897–1931, 365.
196 *Grantham Jnl*, 26 Nov. 1910.

children of the parish in 2017. It had 90 children on the school roll in 2014 aged between 4 and 11, living in Buckminster, Sewstern, Coston, Garthorpe, Sproxton, Stonesby, Wymondham (all Leics.), Colsterworth, Corby Glen, Denton, Skillington, South Witham and Stainby (Lincs.).[197]

Boarding Schools

Revd William Trimmer kept a small boarding school at Buckminster vicarage for a few months in 1823, for young gentlemen preparing for university, but Lord Huntingtower objected and it was forced to close.[198] Mr Rubie opened the Buckminster Commercial School in 1860, offering a range of instruction to day boys and boarders, 'to fit them for the duties of Business', including mathematics, two types of book-keeping, good handwriting, history, geography, Latin, chemistry, drawing and music.[199] The school appears to have failed within a year, and its proprietor was employed by an endowed school in 1861.[200] Another private school was noted in 1873, which was said to be 'efficient in respect of instruction, but otherwise hopelessly inefficient'.[201] This also appears to have been short-lived.

Evening School and Adult Training

An evening continuation school for young men and women was established at the school in 1900 by Alfred Hill, the village schoolmaster. Classes in reading, composition, arithmetic, commercial geography, and the life and duties of a citizen were held on two evenings each week in the winter months.[202] Lord Dysart was a keen supporter, providing prizes and occasionally addressing pupils or leading debates on topics including the metric system and 'Free Trade versus Protection'. There were 12 pupils registered in 1902, increasing to 18 the following year.[203] The date of closure is not recorded.

A training centre for disabled soldiers was established in Sewstern after the First World War, under the auspices of the Ministry of Agriculture, providing a 12-month vocational course including general farm work, market gardening, poultry-keeping and bee-keeping.[204]

---

197 Ofsted Report 2014: http://reports.ofsted.gov.uk/inspection-reports/find-inspection-report/provider/ ELS/119910 (accessed 15 Apr. 2015); Inf. from Kate Parkin, teacher at Buckminster Primary School [2014].
198 Below, 89.
199 *Grantham Jnl*, 23 Jun. 1860.
200 TNA, RG 9/2304/76.
201 TNA, ED 2/272, report Jan. 1873.
202 *Grantham Jnl*, 27 Oct. 1900.
203 Ibid., 1 Nov. 1902, 21 Mar. 1903.
204 Ibid., 21 Feb. 1920.

RELIGIOUS HISTORY

THE PARISH NAME IMPLIES THERE may have been a minster church here,[1] but there is no visible archaeological evidence or extant documentary record before the early 13th century. There was a chapel of ease at Sewstern by 1220. This had fallen out of use by c.1560, and the building had vanished by 1795.[2] Holy Trinity church was built in Sewstern in 1842, and served by the vicar of Buckminster. In an age of declining congregations, causing many rural churches to become redundant, it is noteworthy that both churches remained in use for regular Sunday morning services in 2017.[3]

There was some support for Puritan preaching in the mid-17th century, but no evidence of religious dissent in the 18th century. Wesleyan Methodism and Calvinism emerged in the early 19th century, and chapels were built in both villages. These closed in the 20th century.

Parish Organisation

The seat of the ancient diocese of Leicester moved to Dorchester on Thames (Oxon.) in about the 870s,[4] and was translated to Lincoln in c.1072.[5] Parishes in Leicestershire were transferred to Peterborough diocese in 1837,[6] and to the new Leicester diocese in 1926.[7] The ecclesiastical parish of Buckminster, which included Sewstern, was expanded to include Sproxton and Coston in 1974.[8] Benefice changes in 1984 substituted Wymondham, Edmondthorpe and Garthorpe for Sproxton.[9] Further enlargement in 2005–6 added the parishes of Wyfordby and Saxby with Stapleford to create the large benefice of South Framland,[10] covering nine villages across an area of 6,578 ha. (16,254 a.), cutting across the boundaries of some civil parishes.[11]

---

1   B. Cox, *The Place Names of Leicestershire*, II (Nottingham, 2002), 54.
2   Nichols, *History*, II, 129.
3   *Parish News*, Feb., Mar. and Apr. 2017.
4   A.W. Haddan and W. Stubbs (eds), *Councils and Ecclesiastical Documents relating to Great Britain and Ireland*, III (Oxford, 1871), 129.
5   D.M. Owen, 'Introduction: the English church in eastern England, 1066–1100', in D.M. Owen (ed.), *The History of Lincoln Minster* (Cambridge, 1994), 10.
6   *London Gaz.*, 12 Sept. 1837, 2397–8.
7   Ibid., 12 Nov. 1926, 7321–2.
8   Ibid., 28 May 1974, 6371.
9   *Leic. Dioc. Year Bk*, 1983, 83; 1984–5, 41.
10 *Leic. Dioc. Year Bk*, 2004, 33; 2005–6, 40.
11 Census, 1911.

In 2017, David Cowie was appointed priest-in-charge (rector designate) of the two benefices of South Framland and High Framland, presumably preparatory to the benefices being merged. The latter comprised the churches of Branston, Croxton Kerrial, Harston, Knipton, Saltby and Sproxton. Together, the benefices covered *c.*12,000 ha. (29,650 a.).[12]

Advowson

The earliest record of the patronage is from *c.*1220, when Adam de Bugmenistre presented Baldric to the living as rector, reserving the vicarage to Geoffrey for life,[13] perhaps as a means of providing an income to an elderly priest who had served Buckminster well. The patronage was bestowed on the Knights Hospitaller of St John of Jerusalem in England shortly afterwards, who presented Philip Quentin in 1237.[14]

In 1363, the prior and convent of Kirby Bellars exchanged their advowson of two-thirds of the church at Clipston (Northants.) with the Knights Hospitaller for the full advowson of Buckminster.[15] Following the dissolution of the priory in 1536,[16] the right to appoint a vicar remained with the crown until 1558. In one of the final acts of her reign, Mary I transferred the advowson to Thomas Watson, bishop of Lincoln, and his successors,[17] but this was reversed within a few weeks, on the accession of Elizabeth I.[18] She sold the advowson in 1599 to John Flynt and William Jenkinson of Hardwick (Derb.),[19] who appear to have sold it soon afterwards, as Elizabeth Talbot, countess of Shrewsbury ('Bess of Hardwick') was patron in 1603.[20] John Bewe was presented in 1632 by Christian Cavendish,[21] widow of William Cavendish, 2nd earl of Devonshire (grandson of Elizabeth, countess of Shrewsbury). The advowson was held by William Cavendish, 3rd earl of Devonshire, in 1683, and it remained with subsequent earls (later dukes) of Devonshire until 1826.[22]

Sir William Manners approached William Cavendish, 6th duke of Devonshire, in 1813, wishing to exchange the advowson of Osbournby (Lincs.) for that of Buckminster,[23] and this was finally agreed in 1826.[24] The advowson subsequently passed by inheritance, and was held by Sir Lyonel Tollemache in 1992.[25] Due to a series of local church closures and benefice reorganisations, the patronage was in suspension between 2015 and 2017.[26]

---

12 *Church Times*, 5 May 2017.
13 W.P.W. Phillimore (ed.), *Rotuli Hugonis de Welles*, II (Lincoln Rec. Soc. 6, Lincoln, 1913), 289.
14 F.N. Davis (ed.), *Rotuli Roberti Grosseteste necnon Rotulus Henrici de Lexington* (Lincoln Rec. Soc. 11, Horncastle, 1914), 394–6.
15 *Cal. Pat.* 1361–4, 351; TNA, C143/350/19; TNA, C 143/349/23.
16 *Valor Eccl.* IV, 149; *VCH Leics.* II, 26.
17 *Cal. Pat.* 1557–8, 449; Lincs. Arch., DIOC/BP/CONVEYANCES/14.
18 1 Eliz. I, c. 4.
19 *Cal. Pat.* 41 Eliz. I, 1598–99 (L&I Soc. vol. 328), 26–8.
20 Lincs. Arch., Liber Cleri, 1a/1603, ff. 26d–27.
21 http://db.theclergydatabase.org.uk/jsp/DisplayAppointment.jsp?CDBAppRedID=189055 citing TNA, E 331/Lincoln/8 (accessed 1 Mar. 2015).
22 ROLLR, 17D 47/1.
23 John Rylands Libr., BAG 10/3/26.
24 Buckminster Estate Arch., deeds 158.
25 *Leic. Dioc. Dir.*, 1992, 52. See Landownership for details.
26 Notice of suspension for up to five years dated 31 Jul. 2013 on church notice board, seen 2015.

Income

A division of income between rector and vicar had been agreed by 1220, by which the rector received two-thirds of the tithes of corn, and the vicar received the remaining tithes and all fees, but this may have been a temporary arrangement intended just for the life of vicar Geoffrey. No subsequent evidence exists for concurrent rectors and vicars until Kirby Bellars priory received licence to appropriate the church in 1363.[27] The living was valued at £16 in 1291, the 11th highest valuation in the large Framland deanery.[28] A perpetual vicarage was ordained by the priory in 1363, which provided the vicar with a house, dovecote, barn and orchard, 60 a. of arable land, meadow, pasture, all fees and the small tithes.[29] In 1535, the value of the vicar's living was calculated as £8 7s. 3d., significantly below the deanery mean of £11 3s. 4d., with the rectory (in the hands of the priory) valued at a further £12.[30] Queen Mary's transfer of the advowson to the bishop in 1558 was intended to address the inadequacy of the vicar's income through augmentation from impropriate benefices,[31] but the arrangement was reversed before any change was effected.[32]

The glebe contained 76½ a. in 1605, including 16 a. of pasture.[33] The value of the benefice was estimated at £30 in 1615, when vicar William Lloyd claimed to be 'a verye poor man'.[34] An additional £20 was agreed by Parliament in 1656, to be paid from the impropriate rents and profits within seven Lincolnshire parishes.[35] If this was ever implemented, it was reversed following the Restoration. Income of £73 12s. 4d. in 1708 was derived entirely from glebe land, vicarial tithes and surplice fees.[36] Increasing land and rental values enabled William Bagshaw to let 63½ a. of glebe with the vicarial tithes for £115 annually in 1802.[37] The living was valued in 1825, in connection with the exchange of advowsons, at £218 12s. 6d., comprising £153 12s. 6d. from the glebe, £30 for the vicarage house and £35 for the small tithes,[38] but this appears inflated. The small tithes were commuted for £8 annually in 1842.[39] Total income was £160 15s. in 1851,[40] but the agricultural depression reduced this to £125 by 1890.[41] By 1909, Lord Dysart had augmented the annual income to £300,[42] and it stood at £330 in 1928.[43]

27   *Cal. Pat.* 1361–4, 351; TNA, C 143/350/19; TNA, C 143/349/23.
28   *Tax. Eccl.*, 65.
29   John Rylands Libr., BAG 13/5/2 (18th-century certified copy).
30   *Valor Eccl.* IV, 154–7.
31   *Cal. Pat.* 1557–8, 449; Lincs. Arch., DIOC/BP/CONVEYANCES/14.
32   1 Eliz. I, c. 4.
33   Lincs. Arch., DIOC/TER BUNDLE/LEICS/BUCKMINSTER/1605.
34   A.P. Moore, 'Subsidies of clergy in the archdeaconry of Leicester in the seventeenth century', *Assoc. Archit. Soc. Rep. & Papers* 27 (1903–4), 468.
35   *Cal. SP Dom.* 1655–6, 89; Lambeth Palace Libr., COMM Via/7, 524–5.
36   J. Ecton, *Thesaurus Rerum Ecclesiasticarum* (1742), 316; Lincs. Arch., DIOC/TER/17/14.
37   ROLLR, DE 395/2/22.
38   Buckminster Estate Arch., item 8.
39   ROLLR, Ti/53/1; Ti/279/1.
40   TNA, HO 129/418/99A.
41   *Peterborough Dioc. Calendar, Clergy List and Almanak* (Leicester, 1881), 39; (1890), 40.
42   CERC, QAB/7/4/1/1127.
43   Surr. HC, K 58/15/145, letter 10 Oct. 1928.

Parsonage

The endowment of the vicarage in 1363 included a new house, which was to be built between the south side of an existing rectory house and Hull Lane.[44] By 1605, the parsonage contained three bays of two storeys, and a kitchen with a little house adjoining, of three more bays, with the latter perhaps including what remained of the medieval rectory house. There was also a stable and seven bays of barn.[45] Vicar Samuel Dixon rebuilt the property in 1651,[46] with four lower rooms 'chambered over', a cellar and kitchen.[47] The house had become 'dilapidated' by 1796, with the south wall 'propped up', and the archdeacon ordered that this wall should be taken down and rebuilt.[48] This does not appear to have been effected, and non-resident vicar William Bagshaw declared the house 'ruinous' in 1812.[49] Under some pressure to live in his parish, Bagshaw made plans in 1814 to build a replacement on glebe land almost mid-way between the two villages. The proposed new site was probably suggested by Sir William Manners, who 'highly approve[d] of' the proposed location, well away from Buckminster Park, and offered Bagshaw stone and lime from his quarries, and free carriage of all reusable building materials from the old vicarage.[50]

No records show why that site was finally rejected. William Cavendish, 6th duke of Devonshire and patron of the living, lent Bagshaw £300 interest-free towards the cost of the new house,[51] and he, the bishop or the archdeacon, may have insisted it was built near the church. Thomas Birchnell, a mason of Wymondham, produced a specification and plan for a relatively simple south-facing stone building, almost square in form, with a cellar, three ground-floor rooms and four upper chambers, costing £643.[52] In what appears to be a final attempt to influence its location, Sir William Manners blocked Hull Lane, immediately south of the dilapidated parsonage.[53] Bagshaw responded by rotating the plans, and his new house was built in 1817 on the previous site, but facing the village green to its east.[54]

The benefice was enlarged shortly after the living became vacant in 1983. Buckminster's next minster lived in Wymondham.[55] The former vicarage was sold by the church, and purchased by trustees for the Buckminster estate.

44 John Rylands Libr., BAG 13/5/2 (18th-century certified copy).
45 Lincs. Arch., DIOC/TER BUNDLE/LEICS/BUCKMINSTER/1605.
46 Parish registers.
47 ROLLR, 1D 41/2/111; John Rylands Libr., BAG 13/5/2 (terrier, 1788).
48 ROLLR, 1D 41/18/22, 250.
49 John Rylands Libr., BAG 13/5/2 (licence 10 May 1812).
50 John Rylands Libr., BAG 10/3/30.
51 Lincs. Arch., DIOC/MGA/78.
52 Lincs. Arch., DIOC/MGA/78.
53 John Rylands Libr., BAG 13/5/2 (annotations on very rough sketch, undated).
54 John Rylands Libr., BAG 13/5/2 (sketch plan, undated and mutilated); BAG 10/3/36; *Stamford Merc.*, 4 Sept. 1829.
55 *Leic. Dioc. Year Bk*, 1983, 83; 1984–5, 33, 80.

Religious Life before 1547

There is no firm evidence for a religious house or minster church in Buckminster, but the elevated location of both church and parish, the existence of a chapelry and the church's high valuation in 1291 may hint at early religious importance. This neighbourhood was an area of evangelising activity. Parts of four pre-Conquest crosses survive within a five-mile radius, at Sproxton, Colsterworth, North Witham and Stoke Rochford (latter three in Lincs.).[56] Domesday Book recorded priests in the neighbouring settlements of Sproxton, and Wymondham with Edmondthorpe, and 'half' a church at South Witham (Lincs.). Although neither church nor priest was recorded at Buckminster,[57] it cannot be assumed that there was no church here in 1086.[58]

The first documentary reference to the church is from the institution of Geoffrey as its priest by bishop Hugh of Wells, in 1206–09.[59] The earliest mention of the church dedication is in 1521, when St John the Baptist was recorded,[60] and this remained the dedication in 2017. It is possible that the original dedication was to St Botolph. St John the Baptist's feast day is on 24 June, which was a common date for rent payments in the medieval period, but a monastic cartulary includes six charters of unrecorded date relating to land in Buckminster and Sewstern where rent was due in June, but paid on St Botolph's day (17 June).[61] The day was presumably of significance in the parish. Church dedications to St Botolph are frequently found elsewhere near ancient shire boundaries.[62]

Most of the present fabric of the building dates from between 1250 and 1350, when the patronage was held by the Knights of the Hospital of St John, and the church may have been re-dedicated to St John the Baptist when the building was completed. Three sedilia were created in the chancel in the late 13th century.[63] One of these stalls may have been occupied by the priest who took mass in Sewstern chapel, which is documented from 1220 and will be considered below. Two priests were assessed for the clerical poll tax in 1377,[64] and two priests paid the clerical subsidy in 1526.[65] Thomas Ciston's 1521 bequest for a mass by 'a prest seculer or regular' suggests that Augustinian canons from Kirby Bellars priory or Cistercian monks from Vaudey may have assisted the parish priest at services.[66] Three vestments were recorded in 1552, with one red and one tawny

56   Pevsner, *Leics.*, 384, 431; Pevsner, *Lincs.*, 229–30, 589.
57   *Domesday*, 647, 636, 948, 630.
58   D. Parsons, 'Churches and churchgoing in 1086', in C. Phythian-Adams (ed.), *The Norman Conquest of Leicestershire and Rutland: A Regional Introduction to Domesday Book* (Leicester, 1986), 38–42.
59   W.P.W. Phillimore (ed.), *Rotuli Hugonis de Welles*, I (Lincoln Rec. Soc. 3, Lincoln, 1912), 267; *ODNB*, s.v. 'Wells, Hugh of (d. 1235)', (accessed 20 Feb. 2015).
60   ROLLR, W & I file 1521/23.
61   Rockingham Castle Arch., C1.7.21 F3/10, ff. 51, 51v, 52v, 53, 53v.
62   G. Jones, *Saints in the Landscape* (Stroud, 2007), 47, 112–13.
63   Pevsner, *Leics.*, 116.
64   A.K. McHardy, *Clerical Poll-Taxes of the Diocese of Lincoln 1377–1381* (Lincoln Rec. Soc. 81, Woodbridge, 1992), 15.
65   H. Salter (ed.), *A Subsidy Collected in the Diocese of Lincoln in 1526* (Oxford, 1909), 98.
66   ROLLR, W & I file 1521/24.

silk cope.[67] Ciston also left 5s. to buy 'a prynted masse boke',[68] and it is interesting to note that a parishioner in a rural parish was aware of the existence of printed books in 1521.

Wills suggest a rich religious life within the parish immediately before the Reformation. Two gifts, of 26s. 8d. by John Straker in 1516,[69] and 5s. in 1533 by Thomas Byllysbe in 1533,[70] paid for the rood loft above the chancel arch to be gilded. Alice Ciston left 16d. in 1521 for a painting of St Helen,[71] but mentioned no location. Specific lights or candles were frequently mentioned. John Straker, Thomas Gretham, Thomas Ciston and William Byard left bequests between 1516 and 1528 for the light of our blessed lady and for the sepulchre light.[72] Straker, Ciston, and Ciston's widow Alice each left 4d. to All Souls' light.[73] Widow Joan Byllysbe remembered the sacrament light in 1534,[74] while Robert Lutt left wax for the sepulchre and sacrament lights in 1540.[75] No lights are mentioned by any later testators.

The south chapel of the parish church was almost certainly a chantry chapel by the late 14th century, but no endowment of land is recorded before 1516. That year, Thomas Gretham of Sewstern transferred a messuage and 10 a. of land to feoffees for services of vespers and matins for the benefit of his soul, that of his wife, four family members, his 'good frendes' and 'benefactoures'.[76] He did not specify whether these masses were to be held in Buckminster church or Sewstern chapel. Several others left livestock for 'perpetual' masses, including Thomas Ciston, who requested a sung mass of the five wounds of our Lord in 1521, 15 further masses and another on his year-day, and also bequeathed a cow and four sheep for perpetual masses for himself, his wife, his parents and 'all our friends'.[77] The mention of 'friends' in Gretham's and Ciston's wills suggests there may have been a rural fraternity or guild within the parish. The 1533 will of Thomas Byllysbe left a cow, two ewes and two lambs for an annual mass, and asked for his name to be added to the bede roll, a list of donors whose names would be read out regularly, with prayers offered for their souls.[78] In 1539, Richard Tydd left 16d. for a processioner (a service-book used in processions), perhaps to replace one which had belonged to the recently dissolved priory, and two ewes with two lambs for an annual dirige and mass for his soul and those of his friends.[79] Two chalices, one of silver parcel gilt and one of tin, were recorded in 1552, one of which may have been kept at Sewstern chapel, which is not listed separately.[80]

67   TNA, E 117/11/43/9.
68   ROLLR, W & I file 1521/24.
69   ROLLR, Will Reg. 1515–26, f. 12.
70   ROLLR, Will Reg. 1515–26, ff. 216v–17.
71   ROLLR, W & I file 1521/23.
72   ROLLR, Will Reg. 1515–26, f. 2; Will Reg. 1515–26, f. 102v; W & I file 1521/24; Will Reg. 1526–33, f. 12.
73   ROLLR, Will Reg. 1515–26, f. 12; W & I file 1521/24; W & I file 1521/23.
74   ROLLR, Will Reg. 1526–33, f. 71.
75   ROLLR, W & I file 1540/43.
76   ROLLR, Will Reg. 1515–26, f. 19.
77   ROLLR, W & I file 1521/24.
78   ROLLR, Will Reg. 1515–26, ff. 216v–217.
79   ROLLR, W & I file 1539/103; VCH Leics. II, 26.
80   TNA, E 117/11/43/9.

Sewstern Chapel

Buckminster church had a chapel of ease in Sewstern by *c.*1220, which was to be served three times each week by clergy from Buckminster.[81] It may have originated as a chantry chapel. It was dedicated to St Edmund.[82] It stood in a 1½ a. plot at the west end of the village, presumably on Main Street, with a 1 a. close of pasture abutting on the north.[83] The building may have been in poor condition in 1516, when Thomas Gretham left 3*s.* 4*d.* for its repair.[84] Land used as a smith's shop was left at an unknown date, for a 'lamp' to be kept lit there.[85] A 'chapel-yard' is mentioned in 1586, but the chapel may never have had burial rights: all 16th-century Sewstern residents whose wills left specific instructions for interment asked to be buried in Buckminster.[86]

Religious Life from 1547

Prayers for the dead should have ceased with the dissolution of chantries in 1547, although Richard Loryngton bequeathed 1*d.* in 1549 to every poor person in the parish 'to pray for me'.[87] A cottage which had been left for masses, presumably the bequest of Thomas Gretham, was let for 4*s.* annually in 1549 and sold by the Crown that year to Edward Pease and James Wylson of London, with a piece of land of unspecified size in the parish, which had been bequeathed for a lamp and was let for 12*d.* annually.[88] Enquiries of 1572 and 1573 identified further land given to the church but concealed from the commissioners: the smith's shop mentioned above, another tenement in Sewstern, a close of land, and Sewstern chapel itself. The inclusion of the latter suggests that by the 1540s, if not earlier, this may have been purely a chantry chapel.[89] A manorial court noted in 1550 that the 'parish' of Sewstern had sold the chapel's bell to a pewterer from Stamford without the licence of the king,[90] and this may mark the building's demise as a church. It was still described as a chapel in 1572, but was then 'occupied' by George Leigh for 4*d.* annually,[91] implying it no longer had a religious function. The site was granted to Richard Hill of Heybridge (Essex) and William James of London that year.[92] It was occupied by Richard Askewe in 1586, who claimed it had been surrendered to Edward VI and later granted to him by Elizabeth I. He was ordered to convey the chapel,

---

81   Phillimore (ed.), *Rotuli*, I, 267.

82   ROLLR, Will Reg. 1516–26, f. 102v; TNA, C 66/1083, m. 32; C 78/71/23.

83   TNA, C 66/966, m. 11; C 78/71/23.

84   ROLLR, Will Reg. 1515–26, f. 102v.

85   TNA, C 66/1096, m. 2.

86   TNA, C 78/71/23; ROLLR, Will Reg. 1515–26, f. 102v.; Wills 1566–69/34.

87   ROLLR, W & I file 1549/52.

88   A. Hamilton Thompson, 'The chantry certificates for Leicestershire', *Assoc. Archit. Soc. Rep. & Papers* 30 (1909–10), 564, 568; *Cal. Pat.* Edw. VI, III, 46–8.

89   TNA, C 66/1096, m. 2; C 66/1083, m. 32.

90   TNA, SC 2/183/154, m. 1d.

91   TNA, C 66/1083, m. 32.

92   *Cal. Pat.* 1569–72, 349.

chapel-yard and an adjacent one-acre close (Baylies Close) to feoffees, with the rent to be used for the repair of the parish church.[93]

It has been suggested that Buckminster's vicar Thomas Watson was the Thomas Watson who was appointed bishop of Lincoln by Mary I, who died in 1584, but a 1551 will and inventory for vicar Thomas Watson of Buckminster proves these were different men.[94] Buckminster's Thomas Watson was a married man at his death, and therefore presumably supported at least some reform.[95] Edward VI presented Miles Bens or Bennys after Watson's death,[96] but Mary I presented Matthew Baylye to the living in 1554,[97] usurping Bennys, who launched a suit in the court of Chancery.[98] The outcome is unclear, but a Matthew Bailie was appointed rector of Stainby in 1554, and remained there until his death in 1571.[99]

William Lloyd, presented to the living by Elizabeth I in 1575,[100] lived in the parish, and was 'indifferentlie learned in the latine tonge and scriptures.[101] In 1634, a visitation found the church was using an old and unbound Bible and had no book of homilies.[102] Samuel Dixon was presented to the living in 1641.[103] He was a graduate of Emanuel College, Cambridge,[104] known for its strong Puritan ethos, but was sufficiently flexible in his professed beliefs to continue in office until 1695. He permitted the Puritan and renowned preacher Henry Wilkinson to preach at Buckminster from 1642, and also after Wilkinson was ejected as a canon of Christ Church, Oxford in 1660.[105] Dixon accepted the Act of Uniformity in 1662, and an episcopal visitation that year found nothing significant amiss.[106] He clearly had a good relationship with his patron: following Samuel Dixon's death in 1695, William Cavendish, 1st duke of Devonshire, presented Dixon's son John as his successor.[107] John died in 1718,[108] only a year after his son Edward Dixon had entered Cambridge.[109] The 2nd duke (also William Cavendish) presented John Burman to the living,[110] who conveniently resigned the day after Edward Dixon's ordination, and

93   TNA, C 78/71/23.
94   Nichols, *History*, II, 125; Venn, *Alumni Cantabrigiensis* (Cambridge, 1922), I, 350; *ODNB*, s.v. Watson, Thomas (1513–84), bishop of Lincoln (accessed 12 May 2017); ROLLR, W & I file 1551/91–2.
95   ROLLR, W & I File 1551/91.
96   *Cal. Pat.* Edw. VI, IV, 73.
97   *Cal. Pat.* 1553–4, 41.
98   TNA, C 1/1330/36–38.
99   http://db.theclergydatabase.org.uk/ (accessed 1 Mar. 2015).
100   C.W. Foster, *Lincoln Episcopal Records in the time of Thomas Cooper, S.T.P., Bishop of Lincoln A.D. 1571 to A.D. 1584* (Lincoln Rec. Soc. 2, Lincoln, 1912), 38.
101   C.W. Foster (ed.), *The state of the church in the reigns of Elizabeth and James I, as illustrated by documents relating to the Diocese of Lincoln, I* (Lincoln Rec. Soc. 23, Horncastle, 1926), 43.
102   ROLLR, 1D 41/18/7/ f. 24.
103   http://db.theclergydatabase.org.uk/ (accessed 1 Mar. 2015).
104   J. and J.A. Venn (eds), *Alumni Cantabrigiensis* (Cambridge, 2011 edn), 47.
105   *ODNB*, s.v. 'Wilkinson, Henry (1616/17–1690)' (accessed 9 Apr. 2014); below 99–100.
106   A.P. Moore, 'The primary visitation of Robert Sanderson, Bishop of Lincoln in 1662, for the Archdeaconry of Leicester', The Antiquary, Dec. 1909, 5, 12.
107   http://db.theclergydatabase.org.uk/ (accessed 1 Mar. 2015); J. and J.A. Venn (eds), *Alumni Cantabrigiensis* (Cambridge, 2011 edn), 46.
108   http://db.theclergydatabase.org.uk/ (accessed 1 Mar. 2015).
109   Venn, *Alumni Cantabrigiensis* (Cambridge, 1922), I, 46.
110   http://db.theclergydatabase.org.uk/ (accessed 1 Mar. 2015).

Edward became vicar from 1720 until his death in 1764.[111] He held communion services five times each year in 1721.[112] A description of the church in 1796 mentions the creed, Lord's prayer, ten commandments and 'other scriptural passages' painted on the walls.[113]

Most of the vicars lived elsewhere from the late 18th century until 1834, including William Bagshaw, who appears never to have lived in the new vicarage he built in c.1817.[114] Lord Huntingtower's attempts to persuade Bagshaw's successor William Trimmer that he should also live elsewhere were unsuccessful.[115] Their relationship became irreparably damaged when Trimmer decided to supplement his income by providing a boarding education for two pupils, who practised pistol-shooting on the vicarage land. Angry words passed, and Trimmer later alleged in court that Lord Huntingtower had subsequently caused male and female animals to be placed together in a pound erected on the village green against his property, and had published libels against him. The jury found for Trimmer, who was awarded £2,000 damages, but he was forced to leave Buckminster, appointing a curate before finally resigning his living in 1834.[116] The acquisition of the advowson in 1826 and the death of Lord Huntingtower in 1833 ended this short-term acrimony between the owner of Buckminster Park and the parish's vicars.

James Lawson, presented in 1834, was instrumental in obtaining agreement and raising money to build a new church in Sewstern.[117] Immediately after Holy Trinity church was consecrated in 1842, each church had one Sunday service each week, alternating between morning and afternoon, with Sewstern church attended by many who 'never come to Buckminster'.[118] The religious census of 1851 recorded 44 people attending the morning service at Buckminster and 83 at Sewstern in the afternoon, with the afternoon service always better attended, regardless of where it was held.[119] By 1872, the congregation at either church could reach 200, with c.30 communicants.[120]

The 9th earl (beneficial owner of the estate and advowson between 1878 and 1935) had been baptised a Roman Catholic.[121] Although he joined the Church of England, his views tended towards the Anglo-Catholic end of the Anglican spectrum.[122] Vicar Frederic Blyth, instituted in 1882,[123] supported 'moderate ritual', making 'some addition'

111 http://db.theclergydatabase.org.uk/ (accessed 1 Mar. 2015); J.H. Pruett, *The Parish Clergy under the Later Stuarts: The Leicestershire Experience* (Urbana, 1978), 64.
112 Lincs. Arch., DIOC/GIBSON/12, f. 120.
113 ROLLR, 1D 41/18/22, 250.
114 John Rylands Libr., BAG 13/5/2 (licence 1 Jan. 1818).
115 *Morning Chron.*, 19 Aug. 1829.
116 *Morning Chron.*, 19 Aug. 1829; John Rylands Libr., BAG 10/3/36; ROLLR, 245'50/5, 34; *Leic. Chron.* 7 Apr. 1832; http://db.theclergydatabase.org.uk/jsp/ (accessed 1 Mar. 2015).
117 Below, 97–9.
118 TNA, HO 129/418/99A; John Rylands Libr., BAG 10/3/43.
119 TNA, HO 129/418/99A; HO 129/418/101.
120 Northants. RO, MF 594.
121 *Complete Peerage*, IV, 567.
122 M. Hall, 'Bodley and Garner and Watts & Co's repairs and renovations at Ham House for William Tollemache, 9th earl of Dysart', in C. Rowell (ed.), *Ham House: 400 Years of Collecting and Patronage* (2013), 375.
123 *Peterborough Dioc. Calendar, Clergy List and Almanak* (Leicester, 1882), 39; (Leicester, 1883), 39.

to services to provide 'greater dignity of ceremonial' on festival days,[124] and this appears to have been accepted by parishioners. Celebration of the patronal festival was re-introduced in 1885,[125] and he also increased the frequency of communion services from monthly to weekly.[126]

Church life in the 20th century included a Mother's Union, formed in 1927 when 40 members enrolled, but meetings ceased in 2011, due to declining numbers.[127] In 2017, at least two services, including a Sunday morning Holy Communion, were held in each church every month.[128]

Music and Bells

A gallery was built 'for the use of the singers' in 1730, with John Manners, 3rd duke of Rutland, contributing 5 guineas, and Sir John Hartopp, the non-resident lord of the manor, donating 3 guineas.[129] A strong musical tradition grew in the late 19th century, due to the influence of vicar Francis Rabbetts (1872–82) and the 9th earl of Dysart from 1878, a noted patron of music. An organ by Bevington & Sons of London was donated by Revd Rabbetts in 1872, installed in the chancel and played by his sister, Miss Blagdon; at the same time, a choir was established, with over 30 members, and the singers' gallery at the west end of the church was removed.[130] The 9th earl sent the church choir 'to every good concert within reach', and invited them to sit in the gallery in the Hall when he held musical evenings.[131] In 1885, he provided the church with 'one of the finest [organs] in the midland counties', by Joshua Porritt of Leicester.[132] Installed at the east end of the south chapel, it cost £650, had 33 stops, three manuals and a pedalboard, and remained in situ in 2017.[133] The tradition of a strong choir was maintained until the First World War (Fig. 13).[134] The numbers of boy choristers fell to c.10 by the 1930s,[135] and this trend continued in the later 20th century.

Bequests of 3s. 4d. and 8d. to 'repair' the bells were made in 1516 and 1528.[136] There were three bells in the steeple in 1552,[137] and although none of these survives, the original three-bell oak frame was still in situ in 2014, showing its adaptation in 1657 to receive a new treble given by Richard Hartopp.[138] Two further bells were added in 1873, the gift

---

124 *Grantham Jnl*, 30 Jun. 1888.

125 Ibid., 27 Jun. 1885.

126 Ibid., 13 Jun. 1896.

127 Ibid., 10 Dec. 1927; inf. from Elizabeth Goodacre, former member [2016].

128 *Parish News*, Feb., Mar. and Apr. 2017.

129 Parish register, inserted between 1612 and 1613.

130 *Grantham Jnl*, 7 Dec. 1872; 8 Feb. 1873.

131 *Musical World*, 5 Oct. 1889, 697; *Grantham Jnl*, 24 Jan. 1885, 18 Jun. 1892; 19 Sept. 1885.

132 *Musical World*, 5 Oct. 1889, 697.

133 *Grantham Jnl*, 6 Dec. 1884, 8; the national pipe organ register at http://www.npor.org.uk/NPORView.html?RI=V00050 (accessed 7 Sept. 2015).

134 Inf. from Geoff Dunkley and Ron Skins, Buckminster residents in the 1930s [2015 and 2016].

135 Inf. from Roy Rayson, Buckminster resident in the 1930s [2017].

136 ROLLR, Will Reg. 1515–26/102v.; Will Reg. 1526–33/12.

137 TNA, E 117/11/43/9.

138 County Hall, Buckminster folder (letter from George Dawson, Dioc. Bells Advisor, 11 Mar. 1999); T. North, *The Church Bells of Leicestershire* (1876), 156.

Figure 13 *Buckminster's church choir in c.1902, with Revd Astley Cooper.*

of Revd Francis Rabbetts and his brother, Captain N.G. Rabbetts, in memory of their mother, Harriet Susan Rabbetts,[139] and hung in a new upper frame.[140] Revd Rabbetts also gave the ringers a set of 23 handbells.[141] The Society of Church Bell-Ringers, Buckminster-cum-Sewstern, was formed when the bells were augmented in 1873, under the chairmanship of the vicar. The rules show the strong influence of the belfry reform movement of the early 1870s. There were three categories of member: regular ringers, up to six probationers, and honorary members, the latter being ratepayers or those who 'hold some position', who paid 2*s.* 6*d.* yearly and could outvote the ringing members at meetings through the chairman's casting vote. Only members of the society could ring the bells, except with the vicar's agreement, and the ringers had to agree not to take part in prize (competition) ringing against ringers from other churches. To compensate for this loss, they received an annual distribution from the contributions of the honorary members, after deductions for late attendance and absences;[142] seven ringers shared £5 3*s.* in 1883.[143]

The bells were restored in 1954 and the cracked 5th bell recast.[144] They were still rung regularly in 2015, when the ringers were no longer confined by the rules of the society.

139 T. North, *The Church Bells of Leicestershire* (1876), 155–6.
140 County Hall, Buckminster folder (letter from Dawson, 11 Mar. 1999).
141 *Grantham Jnl*, 8 Dec. 1877.
142 Displayed in church, 2015.
143 *Grantham Jnl*, 19 Jan. 1884.
144 Buckminster Estate Archives, Appeal leaflet (1953); dedication service booklet (1954).

St John the Baptist Church

The parish church, dedicated to St John the Baptist, stands close to the highest ground in the parish, on a site which slopes downhill from east to west (Fig. 14). Built, or rebuilt, in limestone ashlar between 1250 and 1350, it comprises a nave of three bays with clerestory, chancel, north and south aisles, north and south chapels, south porch, tower and spire. Unusually, the tower is above the east end of the south aisle, to the west of the south chapel, making the nave appear very short when the south front is viewed externally.[145] No modern scale plan exists. A plan of c.1795 (Fig. 15) is broadly correct, except that the restoration of 1883 created a vestry within the north chapel, with internal access from the west and south; some windows are also omitted from the plan, but do not appear to be later additions.[146] The maximum internal length of the church is c.79 ft.

The earliest fabric, from the second half of the 13th century, includes the south aisle, large tower, broach spire, three-bay nave and long chancel, but the octagonal piers of both arcades appear to be of c.1300,[147] implying that the north aisle is also of that date.

Figure 14 *The south front of St John the Baptist church, Buckminster.*

145 Pevsner, *Leics.*, 116; NHL, no. 1061281, Church of St John the Baptist (accessed 20 Apr. 2014).
146 Nichols, *History*, II, between 122–3.
147 Pevsner, *Leics.*, 116.

The south aisle has a double-light window with bar tracery of the late 13th century in the west end, a single lancet window to the west of the door (omitted from the 18th-century plan) and a two-light window with geometric tracery to the east of the door, which is taller than an earlier sloping roof line. The chancel has three graduated sedilia and a double piscina in the south wall and an arched tomb recess on the north, all of the late 13th century. Above the recess is a two-light window with Y-tracery, which at some point has been reduced in height. The central pier of the south arcade incorporates a sturdy buttress, helping to support the tower and spire, while the easternmost pier includes supportive walling enclosing the belfry stair. Also from the 13th century, in the churchyard, are five coped coffins, their incised crosses recorded in 1929 no longer discernible.[148] There are no records to show who paid for such an impressive (re) building, but the sale of the manor by William de Bukminster in 1316 realised £400,[149] which appears to have been largely dissipated by 1327, when William de Bokeminster (if the same man) had only the 9th highest tax assessment within the parish.[150]

The windows of the north aisle are of c.1330–50, later than the arcade, and the west window of the nave is of a similar date. Suggestions that the north aisle was extended

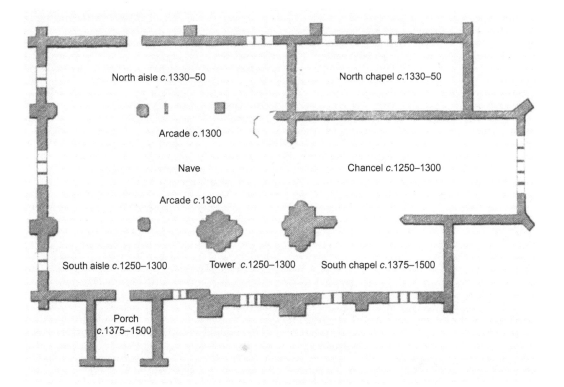

Figure 15 *Development of St John the Baptist church, overlaid on a plan of c.1795.*

148 F.A. Greenhill, *The Incised Slabs of Leicestershire and Rutland* (Leicester, 1958), 60; Nichols, *History*, II, 127.
149 TNA, CP 25/1/124/50, no. 130.
150 W.G.D. Fletcher, 'The earliest Leicestershire lay subsidy roll, 1327', *Assoc. Archit. Soc. Rep. & Papers*, 19 (1887–8), 218.

Figure 16 *A painting of Buckminster church in 1791, looking south-east, from the north side of the nave.*

eastwards in 1883–4 are contradicted by the 18th-century plan, which shows a north chapel, perhaps converted to other uses after the Reformation.[151] This may have been the vestry noted in 1777.[152] It appears to be contemporaneous with the north aisle.[153]

A number of changes were made to the fabric in the late 14th or 15th century. These include the addition of an unusual octagonal turret in the south-east corner of the nave, containing a stone newel-staircase and aumbry.[154] This led to a high platform at the presumed level of the rood loft, with wooden steps giving access to an opening in the pillar for the staircase to the bells (Fig. 16).[155] It may have been used as a pulpit after the removal of the rood loft. A niche faced the nave, but is too shallow for a statute; it may

151   Pevsner, *Leics.*, 116
152   ROLLR, 1D 41/18/21, 248.
153   Pevsner, *Leics.*, 116; *Assoc. Archit. Soc. Rep. & Papers*, XIII (1875), 24.
154   There was a broadly similar arrangement locally at Great Ponton (Lincs.), seen by the author in 2016.
155   ROLLR, Grangerised Nichols, II, facing 127.

Figure 17 *One of the pinnacles on St John the Baptist church.*

have contained a painting and a candle. The south chapel appears to have been built or remodelled at about the same time. The purpose of a small vaulted opening in this chapel within the structural pillar containing the staircase to the bells is unclear.

The south window of the chancel, the sill of which slightly cuts across the top of the easternmost sedile, also appears to be of the late 14th or 15th century. At around the same time, the east window was replaced by a large window of five lights which spans almost the entire wall. The south porch was also added or remodelled at this time, reusing the piers from an earlier porch or doorway at the outer entrance.

The church includes many fine examples of the late-medieval stone carver's art. The porch has three crocketed niches for statues, and both the porch and south chapel have crocketed pinnacles; some of the lower crockets, and the bases of the niches, have been carved as faces (Fig. 17). These blend well with friezes, mostly of faces and foliage, running around the south side of the nave and porch, and on the south side of the clerestory. There are also carved corbels inside the nave and in both aisles.

Externally, the staircase to the bell chamber protrudes on the north-east side of the tower, and unusually extends upwards into the lowest stage of the spire. This gave access to the bell chamber and watch-room, occupied by rota when England was at war with Spain in the late 16th and early 17th centuries.[156] No change in the external stonework can be seen, and it is possible that the church had always had a secondary function as a watchtower. The north-west corner includes an external chimney for the watch-room fireplace.

A blocked doorway in the east wall of the chancel, under an external roof line cutting into the sill of the east window, can be no earlier than the 15th century, but no eastward extension was shown in the 1795 plan.[157] It was possibly the entrance to a vault, although Sir Edward Hartopp's burial place in 1654 was said to be beneath the south

---

156 Above, 12.
157 Nichols, *History*, II, between 122–3.

chapel.[158] There were also two later vaults in the church, where Lord Huntingtower (d. 1833), his widow Catherine (d. 1852), daughter Caroline (d. 1825) and son Felix (d. 1843) were buried before being transferred to the Dysart mausoleum in 1882.[159]

Seating and Restoration

The cost of regular maintenance was partly defrayed by income from three small closes of land in Sewstern, let for £5 12s. 6d. annually in 1706.[160] These were almost certainly Sewstern's former chapel site and lands, or land received in exchange for these, given to the church under the court order of 1586.[161]

There was an 'irregular' mixture of seats in 1832,[162] including Lord Huntingtower's pew in the chancel, with its own stove and 'sides so high that a tall man could only see over them by standing on the seat'.[163] It remained untouched when the church was re-seated in 1854, as did other 'unsightly high pews, made of the roughest deal' in the chancel and at the west end of the nave.[164] There were then no seats in the south aisle,[165] probably to allow access to the vault beneath.

Restoration began with the tower and spire in 1877,[166] at a cost of £300.[167] Lord Dysart asked Halsey Ricardo to survey the church in c.1881 and report on how it could be restored.[168] The report has not survived, and Ricardo's relationship with the earl broke down shortly afterwards.[169] The main body of the church was restored in 1883–4 under architect Charles Kirk of Sleaford. An arch between the north wall of the chancel and the north aisle was opened to provide a vestry, and the chancel arch was raised in height by 6 ft, enabling the whole of the east window to be seen from the west end. A graduated ascent of four steps, including three in marble, was made to the sanctuary, where the floor was inlaid 'with costly Minton tiles', including the symbols of the Evangelists. The plaster was scraped from the walls. The font was moved to the south-west corner, oak seating was provided for 220 people, and oak choir stalls and a desk added in the chancel. The total cost was reported as £3,000–4,000, and was entirely funded by Lord Dysart.[170] A new pulpit, of oak with brass fittings on Caen stone, was added in 1896, in memory of Hon. Frederick Tollemache (d. 1888) and Hon. Algernon Tollemache (d. 1892), brothers of the 8th earl and two of the original three trustees of the estate under the 8th earl's will.[171]

---

158 Ibid., 127.
159 Above, 39–40.
160 J. Broad (ed.), *Bishop Wake's Summary of Visitation Returns from the Diocese of Lincoln* 1705–15 (Oxford, 2012), II, 755.
161 TNA C 78/71/23.
162 ROLLR, 245'50/5, 31.
163 ROLLR, 245'50/5, 32–3; *Grantham Jnl*, 6 Dec. 1884.
164 *Grantham Jnl*, 6 Dec. 1884.
165 W. White, *Hist., Gaz. and Dir. of Leics. and Rutl.* (Sheffield, 1863), 342.
166 Date tablet on building.
167 *Grantham Jnl*, 6 Dec. 1884.
168 Ricardo, f. 336.
169 Ibid., ff. 306–7, 353, 367, 380.
170 *Grantham Jnl*, 6 Dec. 1884; *Kelly's Dir. of Leics. and Rutl.* (1908), 50.
171 Ibid., 14 Nov. 1895; Principal Probate Registry, COW57116g.

St Edmund's Chapel

St Edmund's chapel stood at the west end of Sewstern,[172] but it was 'quite gone and demolished' by 1795.[173] Part of a stone cross, which stood in 'Sewstern-street' in 1792,[174] may once have been outside the chapel. The tithe map and apportionment of 1840 identifies a field in the west of the village, called Church Close and containing 3¼ a., which was then owned by the churchwardens.[175] This may be the site of the chapel, chapel-yard and adjacent close, which Richard Askewe was ordered to transfer to feoffees in 1586 for the repair of the parish church, or land exchanged for these at inclosure in c.1605.[176] There has been no archaeological investigation of this field, but the farmer has noticed nothing unusual there.[177] Another possible site is within the property boundaries of a house a short distance to the east, where a large quantity of limestone has been found, including one carved stone. The owner of this house has reported finding a heavily-worn threshold and a chapel-shaped window (later covered over). The orientation of the present house and its apparent building date suggests that if these were from the chapel, they are not in situ. Two other carved limestone pieces have been found in the garden of a house almost opposite.[178]

Holy Trinity Church

The New Church Commissioners agreed a proposal by Revd James Lawson in 1840 to build a chapel of ease in Sewstern, to be served by the vicar of Buckminster.[179] His grant application to the Society for Building and Repairing Churches explained that Buckminster church could only seat 250 people, and 'nearly a thousand' lived in the parish. They included 368 Sewstern inhabitants who lived 'a long mile' from their parish church. In winter, the road between the villages was 'unsuitable for females, aged and infirm persons'.[180]

Unable to find anyone willing to sell a plot large enough for a church, Revd Lawson negotiated to purchase two pieces of land. The larger of these, on the corner of Back Lane and Stonegate Lane (later Church Lane), was part of a plot owned by John and William Goodacre and measured 14 yd by 10 yd. A further 30 sq. yd immediately to its east was purchased from William Cramp. The site proved too narrow for the plans, and a further thin strip of land, 14 yd by 1 yd, was purchased from the Goodacres. The total cost of

---

172 TNA, C 66/966, m. 11.

173 Nichols, *History*, II, 129.

174 Ibid., engraving between 126–7.

175 ROLLR, Ti/279/1, plot 293 (at SK 885217).

176 TNA, C 78/71.23.

177 Personal communication.

178 Inf. from Penny Vincent and Alan Hart (owners of houses and gardens mentioned), with stones seen by the author [2016 and 2017]. Geophysical investigations of both gardens in 2016, and of the south-eastern part of the nearest field did not reveal building foundations.

179 *Report of the New Church Commissioners* (Parl. Papers, 1840 (640) xxviii), pp. 3–4.

180 Lambeth Palace Libr., ICBS 2807/2.

Figure 18 *Holy Trinity Church, Sewstern.*

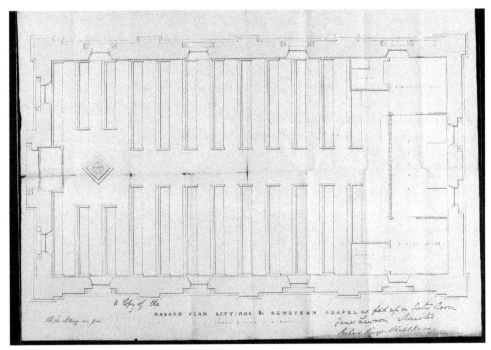

Figure 19 *Salvin's original plan for Holy Trinity Church.*

the land, £85 16s. 9d., was donated by Revd Lawson.[181] Revd Richard Cragg, rector of Wymondham, agreed to donate the cost of the stone.[182]

The architect was Anthony Salvin, whose local work included Harlaxton manor (1831–7), estate buildings at Stoke Rochford (1834), Easton Park (1836) and Belton (1838–9), and St John the Evangelist Church in Grantham (1840–1) (all Lincs.).[183] He produced a Norman revival design which was both attractive and economical: a single door at the west with a bellcote above, a nave and sanctuary, with no chancel or structural division internally or externally, and a stone font shaped like a Norman scalloped capital.[184] Built in ironstone with limestone ashlar dressings, it is Salvin's only known church work in Leicestershire,[185] and the only ironstone building in either village (Fig. 18). The estimated cost was £509 7s. 0d. Through appeals for subscribers, the publication and sale by Revd Lawson of his own poetry and a grant of £100 from the Church Building Society of the County and Town of Leicester, the full amount was raised within a few months.[186] Wishing to retain £100 as a repair fund, a grant was also sought from the Incorporated Church Building Society, which agreed to provide £50. Benches with kneeling boards provided 133 sittings, with the original intention for 30 'private' seats reversed before the building was completed, to avoid creating 'objects of contention' among the parishioners.[187] The church was consecrated in 1842.[188]

The original plans (Fig. 19) showed robing rooms on either side of the altar, a reading desk directly opposite the pulpit, and bench seating throughout the 'nave', including two rows of shorter 'Christening' benches each side of the font, which was directly in front of the west door.[189] The church in 2016 had a vestry area in the south-west corner instead of the eastern robing rooms, and fewer seats.

Protestant Nonconformity

Early Dissent

The Hartopp family, lords of the manor between 1615 and 1763, were early dissenters, but there are no records of any early meeting house in the parish.[190] Archbishop Laud noted in 1633 that the parish contained 'Many Puritans. They go from this parish to Strinsby' (probably Stainby, Lincs.).[191] An account of Puritan Henry Wilkinson's life states that after his ejection from his ministry in Oxford in 1660, 'he lived by the help

181 Lambeth Palace Libr., ICBS 2807/3; ROLLR, Ti/279/1; CERC, 16440.
182 *Stamford Merc.*, 3 Jul. 1840.
183 J. Allibone, *Anthony Salvin: Pioneer of Gothic Revival Architecture* (Cambridge, 1988), 157–65.
184 Lambeth Palace Libr., ICBS 2807/2.
185 Pevsner, *Leics.*, 371; NHL, no. 1360831, Ch. of Holy Trinity (accessed 20 Apr. 2014).
186 J. Lawson, *A Defence of Poesy* (1842); *Stamford Merc.*, 10 Jun. 1842; Lambeth Palace Libr., ICBS 2807/3, f. 6.
187 Lambeth Palace Libr., ICBS 2807, ff. 6, 17, 19–20.
188 TNA, HO 129/418/101.
189 Lambeth Palace Libr., ICBS 2807/23.
190 *VCH Middx* VIII, 183–4, 211.
191 A.P. Moore, 'The Metropolitan visitation of Archbishop Laud', *Assoc. Archit. Soc. Rep. & Papers* 29, (1907–8), 516.

of the brethren at Buckminster … where he exercised his gifts in conventicles'; he died in 1675.[192] By 1686, Sir John Hartopp had moved to Stoke Newington (Middx), and the family may have retained little influence on religious life in the parish.[193] No nonconformist meetings were recorded in 1669, or 1672, and only one man and two women were noted to be nonconformists in 1676.[194] Vicar John Dixon reported no dissenters in 1709 or 1721.[195]

Sewstern Methodist Church

The first recorded nonconformist congregation in the parish met in Sewstern. Its early members recalled a Wesleyan preacher from Carlton (Notts.) speaking at a meeting held in the Sewstern home of Hugh Stevens in *c*.1803. This led to the formation of a congregation and the building of a chapel by subscription in 1808, on land which they failed to convey to trustees. They recorded that their evening meetings began to be dominated by a Calvinist in 1814, who criticised the afternoon's preacher. He refused to leave the group, and was supported by his brother-in-law, who owned the land where the chapel stood. The Wesleyans therefore began meeting separately, in the home of widow Townsend until 1823, when they built a chapel on the edge of the village, immediately to the east of Sewstern Lane, just beyond the parish and county boundary.[196] A large part of the cost was lent by Samuel Veasey, who became the chapel steward, with the debt finally extinguished by a grant of £6 from the Wesleyan General Chapel Committee in 1885–6.[197] The chapel contained 90 'free' and 50 'other' sittings, and held two services on Sundays in 1851, with an average attendance of 60 in the afternoon and 85 in the evening.[198]

In 1903, the growing congregation bought the site of the former Waggon and Horses inn on Main Street, Sewstern from Lord Dysart for £40.[199] Plans for a chapel, school room and offices were prepared by George Camplin of Grantham, and a building contract for £518 was awarded to John Clarke of Sewstern.[200] A grant of £60 was obtained from the Wesleyan Chapel Committee's Twentieth-century Fund, and the building opened in 1904. It contained 120 sittings, 90 of which were free.[201] The chapel closed in the early 1980s, and was converted to a private house (Fig. 20).[202]

192 A.A. Wood (rev. P. Bliss), *Athenae Oxoniensis* (1820), IV, 285; *ODNB*, 'Wilkinson, Henry.
193 *VCH Middx* VIII, 183–4, 211.
194 R.H. Evans, 'Nonconformists in Leicestershire in 1669', *Trans LAHS* 25 (1949); F. Bate, *The Declaration of Indulgence 1672: A Study in the Rise of Organised Dissent* (1908); A. Whiteman, *The Compton Census of 1676: A Critical Edition* (1986), 339.
195 Broad (ed.), *Bishop Wake's*, 755; Lincs. Arch., DIOC/GIBSON/12, f. 118.
196 T. Cocking, *The History of Wesleyan Methodism in Grantham and its Vicinity* (1836), 331–5.
197 Lincs. Arch., Meth. C/Sewstern Wesleyan/3/1, entries for 1824, 1840, 1845, 1871 and 1885–6.
198 TNA, HO 129/427/22.
199 J. Gill, *The History of Wesleyan Methodism in Melton Mowbray and the Vicinity* (Melton Mowbray, 1909), 196.
200 ROLLR, DE 7684/10.
201 ROLLR, DE 7684/11.
202 Millennium embroidery book in Holy Trinity, Sewstern.

Figure 20 *Sewstern's Wesleyan Chapel of 1903, converted to a private house.*

Sewstern Calvinist Church

It is not known how long the evening services which began in 1814 continued. No Calvinist meeting at Sewstern was recorded in 1851, but a congregation was recorded in 1872, and 1882.[203]

Buckminster Methodist Church

It is said that the first Methodist meeting in Buckminster was held in 1833, with early services held in various houses, and in the school room by the 1840s.[204] Evening services, attracting *c.*70 people, were held in a 'Preaching House' in 1851.[205] In 1896 the congregation received notice to vacate the room where they met. Miss Adcock, probably Charlotte Adcock, agreed to sell some land near the old room for a chapel, 'the trustees being unable to obtain a piece of ground in the front street of the village'.[206] The chapel,

---

203 Northants. RO, MF 594, ML 601.
204 Gill, *History*, 197–8.
205 TNA, HO 129/418/100.
206 *Grantham Jnl*, 11 Jul. 1896. Charlotte Adcock was an unmarried head of household 'living on own means' in Buckminster in 1901: TNA, RG 13/3013/26.

built in brick with stone dressings, opened in 1896 and cost £310, including the land.[207] A congregation still met in 1954, but the chapel had closed by 1974.[208] The building was too small to be converted to a private house, and was demolished.[209]

Primitive Methodists

A camp meeting of Primitive Methodists was held in Buckminster in 1867, but there is no evidence of regular Primitive Methodist worship in the parish.[210]

The closest Methodist services for Buckminster residents in 2017 were at Skillington (Lincs.) and Saltby.[211]

207 *Grantham Jnl*, 17 Oct. 1896.
208 Ibid., 5 Nov. 1954.
209 *Leic. Merc.* 22 Aug. 1974.
210 *Grantham Jnl*, 6 Jul. 1867.
211 *Parish News*, March 2017, April 2017.

LOCAL GOVERNMENT

THE TWO MANORS OF BUCKMINSTER and Sewstern were administered as one from at least 1373.[1] The villages were within a single parish other than between 1866 and 1936, although each appears always to have elected its own officers. There were separate parish councils between 1895 and 1936.

Manorial Government

Two courts were listed in 1535, a manor court held by Kirby Bellars priory for 'Buckminster and Sewstern', and a court leet 'in Sewstern and Buckminster' held by the bishop of Lincoln. Both were administered by the priory as a single entity and in 1535, 4s. was paid annually by the priory to the bishop.[2] The bishop's overlordship ended in 1547.[3] Few court rolls survive, but leet courts for 'Buckminster and Sewstern' were held biannually in the 1550s.[4] Each village had its own tithingmen and officers to present offenders. Two field wardens from each village were elected each year to ensure farming by-laws were respected, and a hayward from each village made presentments relating to stray animals and the village pound. Each village also had its own elected constable.[5]

Parish Government before 1894

A town book, commencing in 1665, records the annual election of parish officers chosen from each village. One person from each village was chosen in April or May to serve for a year as both churchwarden and overseer of the poor, and another from each village chosen each December to serve as both constable and overseer of the highways.[6] The liability to serve appears to have attached to particular houses, ensuring that all substantial residents were chosen. Substitutes occasionally acted, and may have been paid by the better-off to perform the duties for them. Robert Gray of Buckminster, for example, acted as constable for Mr Storer in 1674.[7] This was probably Edward Storer,

1   TNA, SC 6/908/20.
2   *Valor Eccl.*, IV, 3, 149.
3   *Cal. Pat.* Edw. VI, I, 153–4.
4   For example, TNA, SC 2/195/79; SC 2/183/54; SC 2/183/95; SC 2/183/55.
5   TNA, SC 2/195/79; SC 2/195/54.
6   Buckminster Estate Office, Town Bk; A. Fox (ed.), *Parish Government in a Leicestershire Village: The Buckminster Town Book, 1665–1767 and Constable's Book, 1755–1813* (Leicester, 2015).
7   Buckminster Estate Office, Town Bk; Fox (ed.), *Parish Government*, 3.

who died in 1712, leaving land in three parishes and goods worth over £250, including engraved family silver and a gold seal ring.[8] Vestry meetings were occasionally called at other times, for example if an officer needed to spend more than 40s. at any one time, or if a levy (tax) needed to be raised from parishioners, set at 1d. an acre in 1718.[9]

The town book finishes in 1767, and later detailed accounts for constables and overseers of the highways from 1755 to 1813 appear to relate only to Buckminster; presumably the Sewstern officers maintained separate accounts, which have not survived. The duties were typical of most parishes. The constables collected national and county taxes and rates, arranged settlement examinations before magistrates, paid for the destruction of vermin, provided cash to wounded soldiers passing through the parish and covered the costs of repairing and maintaining the parish washdyke (for washing sheep), an important asset for a pastoral parish so far from any large stream. As overseers of the highways, the same men were also responsible for ensuring the roads were kept in repair.[10]

Separate accounts for Buckminster's overseers of the poor and churchwardens survive for 1806 to 1839, which also do not appear to have included Sewstern. The work of the overseers of the poor has been described; as churchwardens, they also took responsibility for the church and its services.[11] Although a single rate was levied in the 18th century, by the 19th century each village levied a separate poor rate.[12] As a result, the two townships became separate civil parishes in 1866, under the terms of the Poor Law Amendment Act of that year.[13]

Parish Government from 1894

Under the Local Government Act of 1894, parish councils were to be elected in parishes with populations of over 300, to take over those functions of the vestry which were not directly connected to the church. Buckminster's population at the 1891 census was 328, but Sewstern's was only 203.[14] Under the legislation, Buckminster was entitled to elect a parish council with five members,[15] while Sewstern could either combine with another parish, or resolve to seek the agreement of the county council to have a parish council of its own. Perhaps fearing their residents would only be a minority voice on a joint council, a parish meeting in Sewstern resolved to request their own parish council. The county council gave approval in 1895 to hold elections for five members for Sewstern.[16]

---

8   TNA, C 142/360/44; ROLLR, Wills and Inventories, 1712. Edward's brother Arthur emigrated to America, where he became a noted astronomer, and is named in Isaac Newton's *Principia*: P. Broughton, 'Arthur Storer of Maryland – his astronomical work and his family ties with Newton', *Journal for the History of Astronomy*, 19 (1988), 77–8.

9   Buckminster Estate Office, Town Bk 1718, 1767; Fox (ed.), *Parish Government*, xvi, 37–8, 51.

10 Buckminster Estate Office, Constables' Bk, *passim*; Fox (ed.), *Parish Government*.

11 See above, 73–4.

12 Buckminster Estate Office, Town Bk; Fox (ed.), *Parish Government*, 37–8.

13 29 & 30 Vict., c. 113.

14 *VCH Leics*. III, 184, 198.

15 *Grantham Jnl*, 1 Dec. 1894.

16 ROLLR, CC 3/1/1, 559–60, 564.

The elections to the first parish councils appear uneventful. There is no evidence that Lord Dysart directly influenced the choice of representatives on the Buckminster council, but many of those chosen had a strong connection to the estate, and inevitably almost all would be tenants and/or reliant on the estate for their business. The first chairman was the vicar, Revd Frederic Blyth, who died in 1896 and was succeeded as both vicar and chairman of the parish council by Revd Astley Cooper.[17] The other council members in 1895 were Henry Manners (agent for the estate), Algernon Hack, George Hawley (builder) and Thompson Skins (blacksmith).[18] The five people nominated for the five positions on Sewstern's parish council that year were Herbert Bartram (farmer), William Briggs (carpenter and wheelwright), George Machin (labourer), Frank Royce (farmer) and Thomas Sharp (farmer, post office official and wheelwright).[19] When six people were nominated for Sewstern in 1896, one stood down to avoid the cost of a poll.[20] The Buckminster council met in Buckminster Institute, and Sewstern's council met in the school.[21]

The two parish councils merged in 1936, when Sewstern ceased to be a civil parish, and the merger appears to have been harmonious. The villages were designated 'local needs villages' in 1976, where new housing would only be considered 'on a very limited scale'.[22] In 2015, the parish council had six councillors, and met quarterly in Buckminster.[23] Their powers were limited, with planning applications and major expenditure decided at borough council level in Melton Mowbray.

17   *Grantham Jnl*, 14 Nov. 1896.
18   Ibid., 24 Dec. 1897.
19   Ibid., 30 Mar. 1895, 13 Mar. 1897, census enumerators' books.
20   *Grantham Jnl*, 14 Mar. 1896.
21   Ibid., 14 Mar. 1896, 25 Apr. 1896.
22   Leicestershire County Council, *Leicestershire: Planning for the Eighties* (Glenfield, 1980), 19–20.
23   http://buckminster.leicestershireparishcouncils.org/20552.html (accessed 20 Dec. 2015).

NOTES ON SOURCES

Sources Used

THIS VCH HISTORY OF BUCKMINSTER and Sewstern has been written using a wide range of original documents, some of them printed, but mostly manuscript sources. It is that dependence on primary sources (i.e. created at the time under study) which makes VCH histories both new and reliable. This list includes the main sources used, but is not comprehensive. It should be used in conjunction with the footnotes and the List of Abbreviations. A very important resource is the website of The National Archives: http://www.nationalarchives.gov.uk, which gives access to detailed catalogues and research guides, as well as references to a selection of material held in other record repositories around the country.

Manuscript Sources

Public Repositories

The National Archives (TNA), at Kew holds the records of national government from the late 12th century onwards, with some earlier material, and of some courts. Calendars (brief abstracts) of some of the administrative records of government in the Middle Ages and Early Modern period have been published, and have also been used in this history. The main classes of manuscript documents used in this history are:

AIR 2	Correspondence of Air Ministry
BT	Board of Trade, company records
C3	Court of Chancery, pleadings
C 33 and C 78	Chancery decrees and orders
C 66	Patent rolls
C 134, C 143 and WARD 7	Inquisitions
CP 25	Fines (land transfers)
E 117	Inventories of church goods
E 134	Depositions taken by commissioners
E 179	Taxation, 1134–1689
E 210 and E 326	Ancient deeds
ED 2	School files
HLG 89 and HLG 132	Ministry of Town and Country Planning, Minerals
HO 107	Home Office, Census Enumerators' returns, 1841, 1851
HO 129	Home Office, Ecclesiastical Census, 1851
IR 18	Tithe files, 1836–70

MAF 32 and MAF 73	National Farm Survey, 1941–3
MAF 68	Agricultural Returns, 1866–1988
MH 12	Correspondence of Poor Law Commissioners, 1833–1900
OS 26	Ordnance Survey boundary books
PROB 11	Probate records, Prerogative Court of Canterbury
RG 9	General Register Office, Census Enumerators' returns, 1861–1911
SC2	Manor Court Rolls, monastic houses
SC 6	Manorial accounts, monastic houses
WORK 14	Ministry of Works

The Record Office for Leicestershire, Leicester and Rutland (ROLLR) in Wigston holds records of county administration, records of the diocese of Leicester (from 1926), some earlier archidiaconal records, and numerous parish and private records. The principal classes of documents used in this history are:

Ordnance Survey maps	
1D 41	Leicester archdeaconry records, including glebe terriers (1D 41/2), church inspections (1D 41/18) and subscriptions to the Three Articles (1D 41/34)
17D 47/1	Earl of Devonshire settlement
42D 31/119	Farnham bequest: Sir Edward Hartopp settlement
CC 3/1	Leicestershire County Council, minutes
DE 1841	War Agricultural Committee, minutes 1917–18
DE 2072/111	Duties on Land Values ledger
DE 3538/6	Small schools survey, 1933
DE 3736/box 39	Photographs
DE 8655/103	Photographs
DG 40	Gretton (Sherard) MS
Poll books	
PR/I	Leicester Archdeaconry probate records, 1542–1812
QS 28	Quarter Sessions, crop returns
QS 36	Quarter Sessions, licensing
QS 38	Quarter Sessions, petitions and memoranda
QS 44	Quarter Sessions, licences for Protestant dissenters' meeting houses
QS 62	Quarter Sessions, Land Tax assessments
QS 73	Quarter Sessions, deposited railway plans
QS 95	Quarter Sessions, licences for teachers and meeting houses
Ti	Tithe maps and apportionments

Will and Inventory files, Leicester Archdeaconry, 1500–1603
Will files, Leicester Archdeaconry, 1563–1858
Will registers, Leicester Archdeaconry, 1515–33

The John Rylands Library in Manchester holds the personal papers of vicar William Bagshaw.

Lambeth Palace Library in Lambeth and the **Church of England Records Centre** in South Bermondsey hold central records of the Church of England, including records of the Incorporated Church Building Society, the Ecclesiastical Commissioners and records relating to National (Church of England) schools.

Lincolnshire Archives holds records relating to the Diocese of Lincoln, which included Buckminster and Sewstern until 1837. The main classes are DIOC/GIBSON (visitation returns) and DIOC/TER (glebe terriers).

Northamptonshire Record Office holds records relating to the Diocese of Peterborough, which included Buckminster and Sewstern between 1837 and 1926.

Nottinghamshire Archives holds some records relating to the Cavendish family, earls and dukes of Devonshire.

Surrey History Centre holds records relating to the Tollemache family estate in Surrey, Leicestershire and elsewhere. Most of the estate records were stored in London during the Second World War, when the safe deposit office was blitzed and subsequently flooded by fire-fighting hoses. By the time they were examined, many had been so badly damaged they could not be saved. Those which survived the fire and flood are held in class K58.

Victoria and Albert Museum holds the collections of the Royal Institute of British Architects, which include the letterbooks of architect Halsey Ricardo.

Private Archives

Buckminster Estate Archives holds some of the surviving records of the Leicestershire and Lincolnshire estates of the Tollemache family. The estate office also holds for safe keeping a number of records belonging to Buckminster church (there are microfilm copies of these at ROLLR) and to the parish council.

Belvoir Castle Archives holds the family estate papers of the Manners family, earls and dukes of Rutland. These are not generally available for consultation.

Rockingham Castle Archives holds a cartulary of Kirby Bellars Priory.

Printed Sources

Primary sources

The most important printed sources, including calendars of major classes of records in The National Archives, are included in the List of Abbreviations. The Lincoln Record Society has published many original records of the ancient diocese of Lincoln, which contain information about Buckminster and Sewstern. There are good collections of trade directories for Leicestershire at ROLLR and in the David Wilson library at the University of Leicester, with a selection of the later available online at http://

specialcollections.le.ac.uk/cdm/landingpage/collection/p16445coll4. Local newspapers for Leicestershire and Lincolnshire, and some national titles, have also been used extensively in this research, especially issues of the *Grantham Journal*. Leicestershire titles are available at ROLLR, where there is also online access to many digitised newspapers from other counties.

Books and articles

The county histories published by William Burton (2nd edn, 1777) and John Nichols (1790) remain important secondary sources for the history of Leicestershire parishes, and the Buckminster and Sewstern entries are in volume II of Nichols' *History*. Nichols added original copies of the sketches and paintings used for his engravings within his own copies of the volumes, and this 'grangerised' set is held at ROLLR. The main sources used for architectural history are Pevsner's guide and the Historic England listings.

Databases

The Leicestershire and Rutland Historic Environment Record is available online at http://www.heritagegateway.org.uk/gateway/advanced_search.aspx. For listed buildings, the descriptions held within the National Heritage List for England are available online at https://historicengland.org.uk/listing/the-list. There is a database of Anglican Clergy, 1540–1835 at http://theclergydatabase.org.uk.

ABBREVIATIONS

a.	acre(s)
Assoc. Archit. Soc. Rep. & Papers	*Associated Architectural Societies, Reports and Papers*
Bk	*Book*
Buckminster Estate Arch.	Buckminster Estate Archives, Estate Office, Buckminster
Burton	W. Burton, *The Description of Leicestershire* (2nd edn, 1777)
Cal. Chart.	*Calendar of the Charter Rolls preserved in the Public Record Office* (HMSO, 1903–27)
Cal. Close	*Calendar of the Close Rolls preserved in the Public Record Office* (HMSO, 1892–1963)
Cal. Inq. p.m.	*Calendar of Inquisitions Post Mortem preserved in the Public Record Office* (HMSO, 1904–87)
Cal. Inq. p.m. sive Esc.	*Calendar of Inquisitions Post Mortem sive Escaetarum*, 4 vols (Record Commission, 1806–28)
Cal. Pat.	*Calendar of the Patent Rolls preserved in the Public Record Office* (HMSO, 1891–1986, and L&I Soc., 1998–2014)
Cal. SP Dom.	*Calendar of State Papers, Domestic Series* (HMSO, 1856–1972)
CERC	Church of England Records Centre, South Bermondsey, London
Chron.	*Chronicle*
Complete Peerage	G.E. C[ockayne] and others (eds), *The Complete Peerage of England, Scotland, Ireland, Great Britain and the United Kingdom* (2nd edn, 1910–40)
Dioc.	Diocesan
Dir.	*Directory*
Domesday	A. Williams and G.H. Martin (eds), *Domesday Book: A Complete Translation* (2002)
Farnham	*Medieval Village Notes*, 6 vols (Leicester, 1929–33)
Gaz.	*Gazette*
HC Deb.	*Parliamentary Debates, House of Commons*
Hist.	*History*

Hist. Parl. Commons	*The History of Parliament: The House of Commons* (The History of Parliament Trust)
Inf.	Information
Jnl	*Journal*
L&I Soc.	List & Index Society
L&P Hen. VIII	*Letters and Papers, Foreign and Domestic, of the Reign of Henry VIII* (HMSO, 1864–1932)
Leic.	Leicester
Leics. and Rutl. HER	Historic Environment Record for Leicestershire and Rutland
Libr.	Library
Lincs. Arch.	Lincolnshire Archives
Melton Mowbray BC	Melton Mowbray Borough Council
Merc.	*Mercury*
NHL	National Heritage List for England (https://www. historicengland.org.uk/listing/the-list)
Nichols, *Additional*	J. Nichols, *Additional Collections towards the History and Antiquities of the County of Leicester* (1790)
Nichols, *History*	J. Nichols, *History and Antiquities of the County of Leicester*, 4 vols (1795–1815)
Northants. RO	Northamptonshire Record Office
ODNB	*Oxford Dictionary of National Biography* (online) (http:// www.oxforddnb.com/)
OS	Ordnance Survey
Parl. Papers	Parliamentary papers
Pevsner, *Leics.*	N. Pevsner (rev. E. Williamson), *The Buildings of England; Leicestershire and Rutland* (2nd edn, Harmondsworth, 1984)
Pevsner, *Lincs.*	N. Pevsner and J. Harris (rev. N. Antram), *Buildings of England: Lincolnshire* (2nd edn, Harmondsworth, 1995)
PO	Post Office
Poll Taxes 1377–81, (ed.) Fenwick	C.C. Fenwick (ed.), *Poll Taxes of 1377, 1379 and 1381*, pt I (British Academy Records of Social and Economic Hist. n.s. 27, 1998); pt II (n.s. 29, 2001)
Rep.	*Report*
Ricardo	Victoria and Albert Museum, Royal Institute of British Architects MSS Collection, Halsey Ricardo letterbooks, volume I.
ROLLR	Record Office for Leicestershire, Leicester and Rutland
Rutl.	Rutland
Surr. HC	Surrey History Centre, Woking

Tax. Eccl.	*Taxatio Ecclesiastica Angliae et Walliae auctoritate P. Nicholai IV circa A.D. 1291*, ed. S. Ayscough and J. Caley (Record Commission, 1802)
TNA	The National Archives
Trans LAHS	*Transactions of the Leicestershire Archaeological and Historical Society*
Univ. Leic.	University of Leicester
Valor Eccl.	*Valor Ecclesiasticus temp. Hen. VIII auctoritate regia Institutus*, ed. J. Caley and J. Hunter, 6 vols (Record Commission, 1810–34)
VCH Leics.	*The Victoria History of the Counties of England: Leicestershire*, 5 vols (1907–64)
VCH Lincs.	*The Victoria History of the Counties of England: Lincolnshire*, 1 vol. (1906)

The following technical terms may require explanation. Fuller information on local history topics is available in D. Hey, *The Oxford Companion to Local and Family History* (1996), or online at the VCH website, www.victoriacountyhistory.ac.uk. The most convenient glossary of architectural terms is Pevsner's Architectural Glossary (2010), also available for iPhone and iPad.

Advowson: the right to nominate a candidate to the bishop for appointment as rector or vicar of a church. This right was a form of property which was often attached to a manor, but could be bought and sold.

Agger: an embankment supporting and providing drainage for a Roman road.

Appropriation: the annexation of a church and its tithes to a religious house.

Bailiff: (1) the holder of a public office in certain districts; (2) the agent of the lord of the manor, responsible for administering the estate and collecting the rents.

Barrow: earth or stone mound covering an ancient burial site.

Bovate: one-eighth of a carucate (q.v.), varying from *c.*10–18 a.

Bronze Age: a period of prehistory spanning *c.*2500–800 BC.

Carucate: originally the amount of land a team of eight oxen could plough in a year. This could vary according to the quality of the land, but was typically *c.*120 a. Also called a ploughland or a hide. By 1298, the carucate in Buckminster contained 198 a. This may have included meadow or pasture as well as arable land.

Cartulary: A collection or set of charters; particularly, the large volume, or set of volumes, containing a duplicate copy of all charters, title-deeds, and similar documents, belonging to a monastery, corporation, or other land-owner; a (private) register of charters.

Chantry: in the Middle Ages, an endowment for a priest to say regular masses for the donor's soul, anyone nominated by the donor, or for the souls of members of a guild or fraternity (q.v.), sometimes in perpetuity. Some of the most elaborate arrangements provided for a purpose-built side-chapel in the church. Chantries were suppressed at the Reformation.

Commons: areas of land governed by agreements made at the manorial court, giving specified rights (e.g. of grazing a certain number of animals, or collecting furze) to certain people (e.g. the occupiers of ancient cottages).

Conventicle: a meeting of religious dissenters.

Copyhold: form of land tenure granted in a manor court, so called because the tenant received a 'copy' of the grant as noted in the court records.

Cottar: type of unfree peasant occupying a cottage and a small amount of land.

Court Baron: a manorial court which dealt with tenants' services, agricultural regulation, and transfers of copyhold land on inheritance or sale. It was usually held every three weeks.

Court Leet: a manorial court which dealt with petty law and order and the regulation of agriculture, normally held every six months.

Croft: a piece of land adjoining and belonging to a house.

Customary tenure: unfree or copyhold tenure, regulated by local manorial custom.

Demesne: in the Middle Ages, land farmed directly by a lord of the manor, rather than granted to tenants. Although usually leased out from the later Middle Ages, demesne lands often remained distinct from the rest of a parish's land.

Estate village: a village where all or most of the land and property is owned by one individual or family.

Farm: a fixed annual sum paid as a rent or tax; to hold land or property in exchange for a fixed annual rent; to collect rents, fees or profits due to another in exchange for a fixed annual payment.

Fee: an estate of land.

Feoffees: trustees appointed to manage land or other assets for the benefit of others.

Foreign service: a feudal service due to someone other than the tenant's immediate lord.

Frankalmoign: land held by feudal tenure, where the only service due was to pray for the soul of the donor.

Fraternity: see guild.

Free tenant: a tenant who did not owe services to the lord of the manor.

Furlong: a block of strips in the open fields.

Glebe: land belonging to the church to support a priest.

Grange: a monastic farming complex, usually on land which was remote from the monastery.

Gregorian calendar: because the need for leap years had been miscalculated when Julius Caesar introduced a new calendar in 45 BC, by the 16th century the calendar year no longer coincided with the solar year. Pope Gregory introduced a re-alignment across Catholic Europe in 1582. Britain adopted his calendar in September 1752, when 11 days were lost and the start of the year was changed from 25 March to 1 January.

Guild: in the Middle Ages, either, an urban grouping of artisans or merchants; a voluntary religious organisation whose members were associated in almsgiving, care of the sick, burial of the dead, and in providing Masses for the souls of deceased members.

Hearth tax: tax levied twice a year between 1662 and 1688, assessed on the number of hearths or fireplaces in a house.

Homage: public acknowledgment of the feudal service a tenant owed to a lord.

Houses of husbandry: a term defined by an Act of Parliament of 1597 as a house with 20 a. of land.

Husbandman: a farmer who generally held his land by copyhold or leasehold tenure.

Impropriate: a benefice which has been appropriated (q.v.) to a religious house.

Impropriator: a layman entitled to the church lands, tithes or profits of an impropriated church.

Inclosure: the process whereby open fields were divided into closes and redistributed among the various tenants and landholders. From the 18th century, inclosure was usually by an Act of Parliament obtained by the dominant landowners; earlier, more commonly by private agreement, or by a powerful lord acting on his own initiative.

Inter-commoning: the sharing of common pasture by two communities.

Iron Age: A period of prehistory, defined in Britain as running from *c.*800 BC–*c.*42 AD.

Jetton: a counter used for arithmetic or as a gambling chip.

Kiln house: a building containing a kiln or oven for making malt.

Knight's fee or service: an amount of land capable of providing enough money to provide a feudal lord with a knight for a set period of time – almost invariably 40 days – when required, although some fees demanded other kinds of military service, such as an archer or warhorse. Such obligations became monetary over time, and were abolished in 1662. Smaller estates could be held as fractions of a knight's fee.

Lay subsidy: from the Middle Ages to the 16th century, a periodic royal tax upon the laity, originally assessed on the value of their moveable goods, but by the 16th century also upon property and wages.

Leys: land laid down for pasture in an open-field (q.v.) arable system.

Loculus: burial niche within a mausoleum or catacomb.

Long hundred: appearing regularly in medieval deeds and accounts concerning livestock, the long hundred was six score, i.e. 120.

Manor: a landed property with tenants regulated by a private (manor) court. Originally held by feudal tenure (see knight's fee), manors descended through a succession of heirs, but could also be given away or sold.

Mark: a medieval unit of accounting, worth two-thirds of a pound (13*s.* 4*d.*)

Mesne lord: a manorial lord who held a manor under a higher lord.

Messuage: a house with its surrounding land and outbuildings.

Militia: a military force raised from the general population in times of national crisis.

Minster: originally a religious house of monks, nuns or priests, often at the centre of a lay or ecclesiastical estate. By the 10th and 11th centuries, the word was also used for a church of superior status.

Model village: a village providing a high standard of housing, and often other social benefits, typically built to house the landowner's workforce.

Modus: the conversion of a tithe payment in kind to a fixed annual sum of money.

Open (common) fields: communal agrarian organisation under which an individual's farmland was held in strips scattered amongst two or more large fields, intermingled with the strips of other tenants. Management of the fields, and usually common meadows and pasture, was regulated through the manor court or other communal assembly.

Parish: the area attached to a parish church and owing tithes to it. From the Elizabethan period it had civil responsibilities, hence a 'civil' as opposed to an 'ecclesiastical' parish. At first the two were usually identical, but from the 19th century, when many parishes were reorganised, their boundaries sometimes diverged.

Parliament Roll: official record of the meetings of the English parliament in the Middle Ages.

Pediment: a triangular structure on the face of a Classical building, often above a door, window or gateway.

Perch: small unit of area, containing one-fortieth of a rood (q.v.); also known as a pole, or rod.

Pilaster: a pillar or protruding strip projecting from a wall.

Piscina: a shallow basin near an altar, either within a wall recess, or on a short pillar by a wall, used to drain away the water used by a priest when washing his hands and washing the vessels used in the Mass.

Ploughland: another name for the carucate (q.v.).

Puritan: a Radical Protestant of the late 16th or 17th century, who objected to religious practices which were not supported by the scriptures.

Quitclaim: a document which performs or confirms the giving up of all claims to a piece of property.

Rector: historically, the person or religious house entitled to receive the tithes and other income of a church. Where a church had been appropriated (q.v.) in the Middle Ages, this could be a lay person or impropriator (q.v.).

Rectory: (1) a church living served by a rector (q.v.), who generally received the church's whole income; (2) the church's property or endowment, comprising tithes (q.v.), offerings and usually some land or glebe (q.v.); (3) a house where a rector lived.

Reversion: the right of a previous grantee or lessee to land following the expiry of an existing lease, or on the death of the owner or tenant.

Roman Britain: period from *c.*43–410 AD, when part of the British Isles was governed by the Roman Empire.

Rood: (1) unit of area, important in surveying, containing one quarter of an acre; (2) a cross or crucifix set above the chancel arch in a church, often on a rood loft (q.v.). Roods were ordered to be removed at the Reformation, but replacements were installed in some churches in the 19th and 20th centuries.

Rood loft: a platform, usually of wood, stretching across the western side of the chancel arch in a church, often above a wooden screen separating the chancel from the nave or body of the church. Most were removed at the Reformation, although the steps to the loft remain in many churches.

Scrivener: a professional clerk or scribe.

Sedile/Sedilia: seat(s) for a priest near an altar.

Selion: a strip of arable land in an open field.

Small hundred: five score, i.e. 100; also called the short hundred. The term was used to clarify meaning in a period in which the long hundred (q.v.) was also used.

Sokeman: a type of medieval free tenant.

Stint: the number of animals a tenant was allowed to graze on common pastures, as agreed and enforced through the manor court.

Suit of court: a tenant's obligation to attend the lord's manor court.

Surplice fees: income received by an incumbent for performing services of baptism, marriage or burial.

Terrier: register of the lands belonging to a landowner, originally including a list of tenants, their holdings, and the rents paid, later consisting of a description of the acreage and boundaries of the property.

Tithe: a tax of one-tenth of the produce of the land, which originally went to the church. It could be divided into great tithes (corn and hay), which went to the rector, and small tithes (livestock, wool and other crops), which supported a vicar.

Tithing: a group of (originally) ten householders who were mutually responsible to the court leet (q.v.) for the good behaviour of the whole group.

Tithingman: the elected head of a tithing (q.v.) responsible for reporting any misdemeanours by the members of his tithing or their families to the court leet (q.v.).

Transhumance: The seasonal transfer of grazing animals to different pastures, often over substantial distances.

Turnpike: a road administered by a trust, which covered the cost of maintenance by charging tolls.

Toft: a homestead; the site of a house and its outbuildings.

Tuscan: one of five orders of Classical architecture, distinguished by plain columns.

Vestry: (1) room in a church where clerical vestments are stored; (2) assembly of leading parishioners and ratepayers, responsible for poor relief and other secular matters as well as church affairs.

Vicar: originally a clergyman appointed to act as priest of a parish, usually as assistant to or substitute for the rector. He received a stipend or a proportion of the church's income, such as the small tithes (q.v.).

Vicarage: (1) a church living served by a vicar (q.v), or the income attached to it; (2) a house where a vicar lived.

Villein: In Domesday Book (1086) the villein or villan was a peasant tenant of a manorial lord who enjoyed a freer status and held more land than many other classes of tenant. By the later Middle Ages, villeins were unfree tenants who technically belonged to the lord, usually owing labour services on the lord's land and suffering some other legal handicaps.

Virgate: a standard holding of arable land in the Middle Ages, of quarter of a carucate, generally 15–40 a. depending on the quality of the land. A virgate usually generated surplus crops for sale at market; those with fractions of a virgate probably needed to work part-time for better-off neighbours. Also called a yardland.

Yardland: see virgate.

Yeoman: from the 16th century, a term used for larger and more prosperous farmers, sometimes owning freehold land.

INDEX

CPSIA information can be obtained
at www.ICGtesting.com
Printed in the USA
JSHW022225211219
3115JS00002B/15